SONNETS FROM THE TROPHIES
OF JOSÉ-MARIA DE HEREDIA

SONNETS
FROM THE TROPHIES OF JOSÉ-MARIA DE HEREDIA

RENDERED INTO ENGLISH BY
EDWARD ROBESON TAYLOR

FIFTH EDITION

PRINTED
FOR THE AUTHOR
SAN FRANCISCO
1913

TO THE MEMORY OF
LEVI COOPER LANE
THESE VERSIONS
ARE REVERENTLY
DEDICATED

PREFATORY NOTE TO THE FOURTH EDITION

THE Sonnets here presented are versions of all those contained in Heredia's "Les Trophées." Since the first publication of these versions I have made many changes in them, in the interest of a truer rendering and a better art, while some of the sonnets have been almost entirely recast. That such art as Heredia's can best be exemplified in the French may be conceded; but at the same time it must likewise be conceded that in no language has the sonnet reached greater variety or force, or beauty for the matter of that, than in the English. Indeed, of all the forms borrowed from the French and the Italian, the sonnet form, as has been well said, seems to be the only one that has become deeply rooted in our literary soil. That the task of representing Heredia's sonnets acceptably in the English is truly Herculean may also be conceded; but the very difficulty is a challenge to those who love the sonnet form and delight to work in it; and even partial success in such an endeavor is almost a victory.

In the sonnets of "Les Trophées" the poet never employs more than two rhymes in the octave, his rhyme being, without exception, arranged as follows: abba-abba. In the sestet he allows himself more liberty, about two-thirds of the sonnets having the rhyme arrangement

PREFATORY NOTE

as follows: aabcbc. The rhyme of the others is distributed in a variety of ways, the favorite arrangement being aabccb. It is worthy of note that the rhyme arrangement of the sestet abcabc, which is so frequently found in the English-written sonnet, is employed by him but once. In several instances he uses but two rhymes in the sestet, and occasionally he closes it with a couplet. In the versions here presented the form of the originals, including the rhyme arrangement, has been strictly followed. In several of the versions but two rhymes in the sestet have been employed instead of the three of the original; but in these instances the arrangement of the rhyme is the same as that of the original—that is, the lines rhyme in the same way, only fewer rhymes are employed. All of these versions are written in the pentameter in which the English sonnet is almost universally written.

For a penetrating and masterly study of the

PREFATORY NOTE

(October 3, 1905), many articles have been written about him in Europe and America, with no dissent, so far as I know, in the matter of the high and unique quality of his sonnets.

Since the publication of the third edition, now out of print, I have again with great care gone over the work with the necessary result of making a number of changes and of adding some more notes. I dare not say, even now, that my work is final. My feeling in this regard is fairly well represented by the sonnets entitled "The Passion for Perfection" and "The Music of Words," copies of which I have ventured to print in this volume, and which, as there placed, I trust will not be considered by the judicious as an impertinence.

E. R. T.

San Francisco
September 23, 1906.

xii

CONTENTS

	Page
Prefatory Note to the Fourth Edition	ix
Prefatory Note to the Fifth Edition	xii
The Passion for Perfection	xix
The Music of Words	xxi
To José-Maria de Heredia	1

GREECE AND SICILY

Oblivion	3
Hercules and the Centaurs	7
Nemea	9
Stymphalus	10
Nessus	11
The Centauress	12
Centaurs and Lapithae	13
Flight of the Centaurs	14
The Birth of Aphrodite	15
Jason and Medea	16
The Thermodon	17
Artemis and the Nymphs	19
Artemis	21
The Chase	22
Nymphaea	23
Pan	24
The Bath of the Nymphs	25
The Vase	27
Ariadne	28
Bacchanal	29
The Awakening of a God	30
The Magician	31
The Sphinx	32
Marsyas	33

CONTENTS

Tepidarium	70
Tranquillus	71
Lupercus	72
The Trebia	73
After Cannae	74
To a Triumpher	75
Antony and Cleopatra	77
The Cydnus	79
Evening of Battle	80
Antony and Cleopatra	81
Epigraphic Sonnets	83
The Vow	85
The Spring	86
The Beech-Tree God	87
To the Divine Mountains	88
The Exiled	89

THE MIDDLE AGE AND THE RENAISSANCE

A Church Window	93
Epiphany	94
The Wood-worker of Nazareth	95
A Medal	96
The Rapier	97
After Petrarch	98
On the Book of Loves of Pierre de Ronsard	99
The Beautiful Viole	100
An Epitaph	101
Gilded Vellum	102
The Dogaressa	103
On the Old Bridge	104
The Old Goldsmith	105

xvi

CONTENTS

The Sea of Brittany	139
A Painter	141
Brittany	142
A Flowery Sea	143
Sunset	144
Star of the Sea	145
The Bath	146
Celestial Blazon	147
Armor	148
A Rising Sea	149
A Sea Breeze	150
The Shell	151
The Bed	152
The Eagle's Death	153
More Beyond	154
The Life of the Dead	155
To the Tragedian E. Rossi	156
Michelangelo	157
On a Broken Marble	158
Heredia Dead	161
Notes:	
Nemea	165
Centaurs and Lapithae	165
The Awakening of a God	165
The Magician	165
Marsyas	166
Regilla	167
The Charioteer	169
For Virgil's Ship	171
To Sextius	172
God of the Gardens — V	172

xviii

THE PASSION FOR PERFECTION

What deep desires are ours, what searching pains,
To find the word we so supremely need;
To frame a diction worthy Art's great meed,
That winged with music bears immortal strains!

Our thought when bound in rhythm oft contains
Such teasing imperfections, that we feed
The hours in their cure, then inly bleed,
For fear some vexing blemish yet remains.

Dear nymph, Perfection, how thou dost elude
Thy fond pursurer!—seeming near, then far,
Enticing ever with allurement sweet,

Till after trial many a time renewed,
He sees thee blaze a solitary star
In some high, inaccessible retreat.

THE MUSIC OF WORDS

(Tennyson said in one of his talks that "People do not understand the music of words.")

To give to Beauty her immortal meed
As gemmed she lies immaculately fair;
To paint the hopes that end in fell despair,
While tones mellifluous every passion feed;

To follow Fancy's fairy troop that lead
Though vales of Dream embathed in drowsèd air,
Or on Imagination's heights to dare,
What nectar-hearted, golden words we need—

Such words as thine, thou muse-encrownèd one,
Who, like some inextinguishable sun,
Shall light the heavens of man forevermore;

Such words as Homer sent, long, long ago,
With music winged, through Hellas' heart of woe,
Or such as deathless make Heredia's lore.

"All ancient glory sleeps, and men forget,
Unless there comes the poet with his art,
The flower of arts; and pouring from his tongue
A mingled stream of wisdom, verse and song,
Records great deeds in strains that never die."
    (From Pindar's sixth Isthmian Ode
      as translated by Hugh Seymour Tremenheere.)

"For the thing that one hath well said goeth forth with a voice unto everlasting; over fruitful earth and beyond the sea hath the light of fair deeds shined unquenchable forever."
    (From Pindar's third Isthmian Ode
      as translated by Ernest Myers.)

    "Les dieux eux-mêmes meurent,
    Mais les vers souverains
        Demeurent
    Plus fort que les airains."
      (Théophile Gautier.)

The Cities vanish; one by one
The glories fade that paled the sun;
At Time's continuous, fateful call
The palaces and temples fall;
While Heroes do their deeds and then
Sink down to earth as other men.
Yet, let the Poet's mind and heart
But touch them with the wand of Art,
And lo! they rise and shine once more
In greater splendor than before.

TO JOSÉ-MARIA DE HEREDIA

'Twas eagle-winged, imperial Pindar who
Sent down the ages on the tide of song
The thought that only to the years belong
Those deeds that win immortal poet's due.

Still rise his crownèd athletes to the view,
On his unwearied pinions borne along;
Still shepherd's pipe and lay sound sweet and strong
As when Theocritus attuned them true.

And so through thee the feats of heroes great,
The hues of life of other times than ours,
With such refulgence in thy sonnets glow,

That in the splendor of their new estate,
They there, with deathless Art's supernal powers,
Shall o'er the centuries enchantment throw.

San Francisco,
May 31, 1897.

GREECE AND SICILY

OBLIVION

THE Temple's ruins all the headland strew,
Upon whose tawny height brass heroes wane,
With marble goddesses, whose glory vain
The lonely grass shrouds tenderly from view.

Only at times a careless herdsman, who,
Leading his drove to drink, pipes an old strain
Which floods the heavens to the very main,
Shows his dark form against the boundless blue.

The Earth, sweet mother to the Gods of old,
At springtime vainly, eloquently weaves
Round the rent capital acanthus leaves;

But man, no more by ancient dreams controlled,
Hears without tremor, in the midnight deep,
The grieving Sea for her lost sirens weep.

HERCULES AND THE CENTAURS

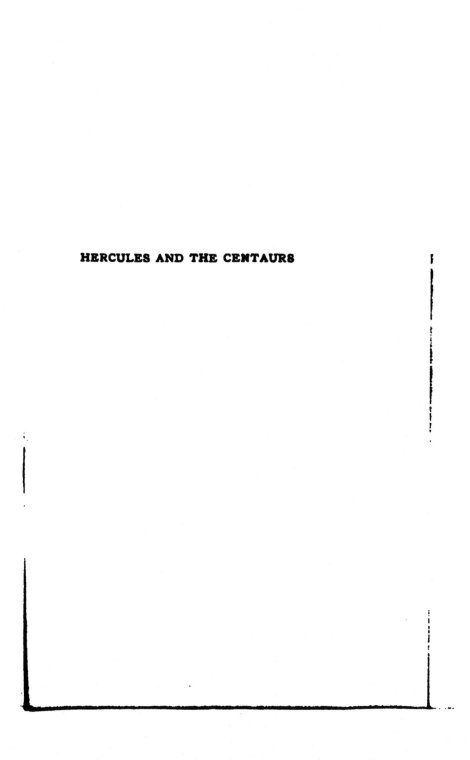

HERCULES AND THE CENTAURS

NEMEA

SINCE the lone Tamer in the forest drear
Made bold to search for every frightful trace,
Resounding roars have told the fierce embrace.
Now sinks the sun, and silence lulls the ear.

The herdsman toward Tirynthus flees in fear
Through thicket, brier and brake with quickening pace,
And sees, with eyes bulged from their orbits' space,
The tawny monster at the wood's edge rear.

He screams. He Nemea's awful terror saw,
That 'gainst the blood-red sky its armèd jaw,
Disheveled mane and tusks malignant shows;

For then mysterious twilight creeping in,
Great Hercules, round him the floating skin,—
Man blent with beast,—a grewsome hero grows.

See note p. 165.

10

HERCULES AND THE CENTAURS

NESSUS

WHEN I of life had but my brothers' share,
The better things or deeper ills unknown,
My roving rule Thessalian hills did own,
Whose icy torrents laved my ruddy hair.

Thus in the sun I grew, free, happy, fair;
And day or night nought vexed me, save alone
When to my nostrils' eager breath was blown
The ardent scent of the Epirus mare.

But since the mighty archer's spouse I've seen
Smiling triumphantly his arms between,
My hairs are bristled and desires torment;

For that some God, in his accursèd plan,
Has in my loins' too feverous blood all blent
The lust of stallion with the love of man.

12

HERCULES AND THE CENTAURS

CENTAURS AND LAPITHÆ

NOW rushes to the feast the nuptial tide—
Centaurs and warriors drunken, bold and fair;
And flesh heroic, in the torches' glare,
Immingles with the Cloud's sons' tawny hide.

Jests, tumult... Screams... 'Gainst black-haired
    breast the Bride,
Her purple rended, struggles in despair,
To hoofs' hard blows the bronze rings through the air,
While crashes down the table in its pride.

Then one upsprings to whom the mightiest bow;
A lion's muffle frowns upon his brow,
Bristling with hairs of gold. 'Tis Hercules.

Whereat, from end to end of that vast space,
Cowed by the fury of his wrathful face,
The monstrous, guilty troop, loud snorting, flees.

See note p. 165.

14

THE BIRTH OF APHRODITE

UNBOUNDED Chaos wrapped the worlds of old
Where ranged all measureless both Time and Space,
Till Gæa, bounteous to her Titan race,
Gave them her fecund breasts of wealth untold.

They fell. The Stygian waves above them rolled,
And storm-swept never had the Spring's fair face
Brightened to feel the blazing sun's embrace,
Nor Summer seen her harvest's fruited gold.

In savage state, no joys within their breast,
The immortals held Olympus' snowy crest.
But from the heavens the virile dew fell free;

The Ocean cleaved; and Aphrodite nude
Rose radiant from the foaming, glowing sea
With life's own blood of Uranus endued.

16

THE THERMODON

ToWARD Themiscyra which in dire despair
Has shaken all day with clash of horsemen dread,
Dark, doleful, slow, Thermodon bears the dead,
The arms, the chariots, no more to dare.

Philippis, Phœbe, Marpe, Aella, where?
Hippolyté and Asteria who led
The royal host to slaughter's gory bed?
Their pale, disheveled bodies now lie there.

Such giant lily bloom is here laid low,
High-heaped the warriors all the shores bestrow,
Where madly neighs at times some struggling horse;

And the Euxine sees at dawn far up the flood
Ensanguined, from its mouth unto its source,
White stallions flying red with virgins' blood.

ARTEMIS AND THE NYMPHS

ARTEMIS

As these wood-odors every place rise o'er,
Thy nostrils wide dilate, thou huntress bright,
And in thy virginal and virile might,
Thy locks thrown back, thou settest out once more.

And now with leopards' hoarse, incessant roar
Thou mak'st Ortygia's isle resound till night,
As through the orgies' reek thou leapest light,
Where mangled hounds imbrue the grass with gore.

But most thou joyest, Goddess, when the brier
Bites thee, and tooth or claw tears with fell ire
Thy glorious arms whose shaft revenge has ta'en;

For thy heart would the cruel sweetness dare
Of mingling an immortal purple there
With black and hideous blood of monsters slain.

ARTEMIS AND THE NYMPHS

THE CHASE

THE chariot to the horses' flying feet
Heaven's summit mounts, their hot breath making glow
The golden plains that undulate below;
And Earth lies basking in the flaming heat.

In vain the forest's leaves in masses meet:
The Sun, where hazy peaks their glories show,
In shade where silvery fountains laughing flow,
Steals, darts and glints, in victory complete.

'Tis the hour flamboyant when, through brake and brier,
Bounding superb with her Molossians dire
Mid blood and death, with cries of clamor's brood,

Her arrows flying from the tightened string,
With streaming locks, the breathless, conquering,
Distracted Artemis affrights the wood.

ARTEMIS AND THE NYMPHS

NYMPHÆA

In westward flight the car of heavenly mould
Speeding toward the horizon's verge, in vain
The powerless God pulls back with fourfold rein
His horses plunging in the glowing gold.

It sinks. The sea's hoarse voice in moaning told
Fills the empurpling heavens with sad refrain,
While silently mid evening's tranquil train
The Crescent in her silvery garb is stoled.

'Tis now the time when Nymphs, where springs gush clear,
Throw the slack bow the empty quiver near.
Except a stag's far belling, all is still.

The dance whirls on beneath the moon's warm ray,
Where Pan, with slackening then with hurried play,
Laughs as the reeds at his own breathing thrill.

ARTEMIS AND THE NYMPHS

THE BATH OF THE NYMPHS

From the Euxine sheltered is a vale where grows
Above the spring a leaning laurel tree,
Wherefrom a pendent Nymph in frolic glee
Touches the gelid pool with timorous toes.

Her sisters, challenged by the shells where flows
The gushing wave they sport with joyously,
Plunge deep, and from the foam a hip gleams free,
And from bright locks, a bust or bosom's rose.

The great, dark wood is filled with mirth divine.
Sudden, two eyes within the shadow shine.
The Satyr 'tis! . . . His laugh benumbs their play;

And forth they dart. So, at a crow's ill cry,
Cayster's snowy swans in wild array
Above the river all distracted fly.

THE VASE

A HAND most cunning cut this ivory piece;
Here Colchis' forests are, while here combine
Brave Jason, with Medea of eye malign,
And on a stela's top the glittering Fleece.

The Nile, great source, flows here without surcease,
Near where Bacchantes, nectar-mad, entwine
The yoke of bulls with foliage-gloried vine,
While some essay the heavy yokes' release.

Beneath, are cavaliers that hack and slay,
The dead upon their bucklers borne away,
The mothers' tears, the old with doleful gaze;

For handles apt, Chimæras who, with breast
Robust and white against the edges pressed,
Forever drink from the exhaustless vase.

28

BACCHANAL

Loud clamors fill the Ganges with affright:
The tigers from their yokes have torn away,
And, fiercely mewing, bound; while in dismay
Bacchantes crush the vintage in their flight.

The fruited vines, mangled by claw and bite,
Spatter the striped ones with their reddening spray
Near where the leopards, leaping to the fray,
Roll in the purple mire their bellies white.

The beasts all dazed, whose bodies writhe and tear
As roar on roar with growl long-drawn is rolled,
Snuff blood still richer through their tawny gold;

But the mad God, shaking his thyrsus there,
Cheers the strange sport, and adds unto the bale
The howling female with the roaring male.

THE AWAKENING OF
A GOD

WITH bruisèd throat, their tresses flowing free,
Their grieving goaded by the tears that rise,
The Byblus women with lugubrious cries
Conduct the slow and mournful obsequy.

For on the couch, heaped with anemone,
Where death has closed his languishing, large eyes,
Perfumed with spices and with incense lies
The one by Syria's maids loved doatingly.

The singers sound the dirge till morning breaks.
But look! Now at Astarte's call he wakes —
Mysterious Spouse by whom the myrrh's bedewed.

He's risen, the youth of old! and all the heaven
Blossoms in one great rose with blood bright-hued
Of an Adonis to celestials given.

See note p. 165.

THE MAGICIAN

EACHWHERE, even at the altars I embrace,
She calls, her pleading arms my vision fill.
O sire revered, O mother, who did will
To bear me, am not I of hateful race?

The Eumolpid vengeful one in Samothrace
Shakes not his red robes at my threshold, still
I fly faint-hearted, leaden-footed, till
I hear the sacred dogs howl on my trace.

In every spot to wretched me are nigh
The black enchantments, hateful, sinister,
That all the wrathful Gods have bound me by;

For they have irresistibly armed her
Intoxicating mouth and deep dark eye,
To slay me surely with her kiss and tear.

See note p. 165.

32

MARSYAS

THY natal pines which raptured heard thy strains
Burnt not thy flesh, O thou to woes decreed!
Thy bones are shattered, and thy blood-drops feed
The flood the Phrygian Mount pours toward the plains.

The pride-blown Citharist, who jealous reigns,
Has with his plectrum riven thy every reed,
That taught the birds and tamed the lion's breed;
And of Celæna's singer nought remains—

Nought but a bloody shred on yonder yew
Where the poor wretch his nameless horror knew.
O cruel God! O cries of that sweet voice!

Beneath a hand too wise no more you'll find
Mæander's stream the sighing flute rejoice,
For Marsyas' skin is plaything of the wind.

See note p. 166.

PERSEUS AND ANDROMEDA

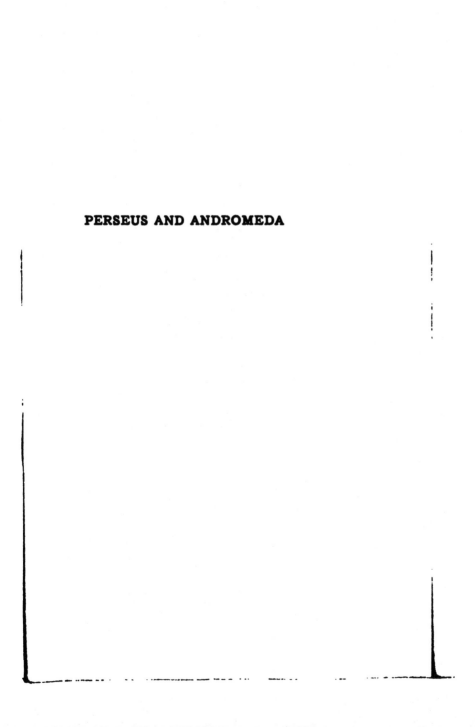

PERSEUS AND ANDROMEDA

ANDROMEDA GIVEN TO THE MONSTER

CEPHEUS' chaste one, alas! disheveled, lone,
Chained to the island rock of sunless gloom,
Writhing and sobbing, mourns in hopeless doom
Her regal form that terror makes its own.

The monstrous ocean, by the tempest blown,
Spatters her icy feet with biting spume,
While everywhere before her closed eyes loom
The gaping jaws in myriad horror shown.

Like peal of thunder from a cloud-free sky
A sudden neighing rolls and echoes nigh.
Her eyes fly open. Fear and joy are one;

For she beholds, in whirling flight and free,
The wingèd horse, upbearing Zeus's son,
Stretch his grand shade of azure on the sea.

38

THE RAVISHMENT OF ANDROMEDA

The splendid wingèd horse, in noiseless flight,
From out his nostrils blowing clouds of fume,
Bears them, with quivering of his every plume,
Across the starry ether and blue night.

Now Afric plunges from their soaring height,
Then Asia . . . desert . . . Libanus in tomb
Of mist and fog . . . and here, all white with spume,
The mystic sea that closed sweet Helle's sight.

Like two enormous cloaks the wind swells wide
The pinions which, as through the stars they glide,
Keep the clasped lovers nested from the cold;

While, as their throbbing shadows they descry,
From Aries to Aquarius they behold
Their Constellations dawning in the sky.

EPIGRAMS AND BUCOLICS

EPIGRAMS AND BUCOLICS

THE GOATHERD

Pursue, O shepherd, in this gorge no more
That bounding, stupid goat; for on the side
Of Mænalus, where summer bids us bide,
Night rises quickly, so thy hope give o'er.

Rest here; of figs and wine I've ample store.
All day this wild retreat have we espied.
Speak low, Mnasylus, Gods roam far and wide
And Hecate's eyes this very spot explore.

A Satyr's cave is yon dark gap below—
Familiar demon whom these summits know.
Be still and he may come from out his nook.

Dost hear the pipe that sings upon his lip?—
'Tis he! His horns now catch the rays; and look,
He makes my charmed goats in the moonlight trip.

44

EPIGRAMS AND BUCOLICS

VOTIVE EPIGRAM

To Ares stern! To Eris strife-possessed!
Help me, I'm old, to give this pillar these:
My shield, my sword well hacked with braveries,
My broken helmet with its bloody crest.

Join there this bow. But, say, is't meet I rest
The hemp around the wood,— hard medlar tree's
No arm but mine has ever bent with ease,—
Or stretch the cord again with eager zest?

The quiver also take. Thine eye cons o'er
The sheath of leather for the archer's store—
The arrows which the wind of battle floats.

'Tis empty; and thou think'st my shafts are gone?
Then hie thee to the field of Marathon,
Where thou wilt find them in the Persians' throats.

46

THE SHIPWRECKED ONE

With breeze astern, and sky serenely clear,
He parts from Egypt at Arcturus' rise,
And as the Pharos fades before his eyes
His brass-lined, speedy ship fills him with cheer.

But Alexandria's mole no more he'll near:
In waste of sand not e'en the young kid tries
The tempest's hand has scooped his grave, where sighs
A wind-entwisted shrub all lone and drear.

In fold the deepest of the shifting dune,
In dawnless night where shines nor star nor moon,
As last the navigator quiet owns.

O Earth, O Sea, pity his anxious Shade!
And on the Hellenic shore where rest his bones
Thy tread be light, thy voice be silent made.

EPIGRAMS AND BUCOLICS

THE PRAYER OF THE DEAD

STOP!—Traveller, list to me. If thy step run
To Cypselus and to the Hebrus' shore,
Old Hyllus find and pray him to deplore
Without surcease his unreturning son.

My murdered flesh the ravenous wolves have won;
The rest in this dark thicket lies; and o'er
The Erebus-gloomed banks great shadows pour
Indignant tears. My death's avenged by none.

Depart then; and shouldst thou, when dies the day,
See at the grave's or hillock's foot delay
A black-veiled woman reft of every bloom,

Approach; nor night nor charms need give thee fears;
For 'tis my mother, who, on shadowy tomb,
Clasps a void urn and fills it with her tears.

EPIGRAMS AND BUCOLICS

THE SLAVE

Naked and wretched, with the vilest cheer,
Such slave am I — my body bears the signs —
Born free upon the gulf whose beauty shines
Where Hybla's honeyed slopes their summits rear.

Alas! I left the happy isle . . . Ah! shouldst thou steer
Thy course to Syracuse's bees and vines,
Following the swans as winter's cold declines,
Good host, acquaint thee with my lovèd dear.

Shall I ne'er see her pure, deep-violet eye
Reflecting, brimmed with smiles, her natal sky
Beneath her dark-hued brow's victorious bow?

Have pity!— Find my Clearista, pray;
Tell her I live once more her face to know;
Thou canst not miss her, for she's sad alway.

50

EPIGRAMS AND BUCOLICS

TO HERMES CRIOPHORUS

THAT the companion of the Naiads may
Be pleased the ewe anear the ram to lead,
So that might endless multiply the seed
Of browsing flocks that on Galæsus stray,

He should be gladdened by the feast's array
Beneath the herdsman's canopy of reed,
For sweet to Pan his sacrificial meed
On marble table or on block of clay.

Then honor Hermes, for the God so wise
Prefers pure hands whereby the victim dies
To splendor's wealth of altar or of fane.

Friend, raise on border of thy mead a mound,
And with the blood of hairy goat there stain
The turf with purple and imbrue the ground.

52

REGILLA

A<small>NNIA</small> Regilla, Aphrodite's own
And Ganymede's, in death reposes here—
Æneas' daughter to Herodes dear.
So beauteous, happy, young, for her make moan.

The Shade, whose lovely body here lies lone,
In the Blest Isles with him who rules austere
Counts all the days, the months, and long, long year,
Since banished far from all that she had known.

Her memory haunts her spouse, and unconsoled,
On purple bed of ivory and gold
He sleepless tosses and lamenting cries.

He yet delays. He comes not. And the dear's
Lorn spirit, filled with anxious hope, still flies
Round the black sceptre Rhadamanthus rears.

See note p. 167.

54

EPIGRAMS AND BUCOLICS

THE CHARIOTEER

STRANGER, that one who treads the golden pole,
His steeds of black, in one hand fourfold rein,
The other holding whip of ashen grain,
Better than Castor can his car control.

His father's not so high on glory's roll . . .
But see, he starts, the limit red to gain,
And strews his rivals o'er the arena's plain—
This Libyan bold dear to the Emperor's soul.

Round the dazed circus toward the goal and palm
Seven times the victor, dizzy yet still calm,
Has whirled. All Hail, son of Calchas the Blue!

And thou mayst see (if that a mortal eye
The heaven-crowned car with wings of fire may view)
Once more to Porphyry glorious Victory fly.

See note p. 169.

56

ROME AND THE BARBARIANS

ROME AND THE BARBARIANS

FOR VIRGIL'S SHIP

MAY your kind stars guard well all dangers through,
Bright Dioscuri, Helen's kin divine,
The Latin poet who would fain see shine
The golden Cyclades amid the blue.

May he have softest airs man ever knew;
May perfume-breathed Iapyx now incline
With swelling sail to speed him o'er the brine,
Until the stranger shore shall glad his view.

Through all the islands where the dolphins glide
The Mantuan singer fortunately guide;
Lend him, O Cygnus' sons, fraternal ray.

One-half my soul the fragile boat contains,
Which o'er the sea that heard Arion's lay
Bears glorious Virgil to the Gods' domains.

See note p. 171.

ROME AND THE BARBARIANS

A LITTLE VILLA

YES, that's the heritage of Gallus hoar
Thou dost on yon cisalpine hill descry;
A pine his humble house is sheltered by,
Whose lowly roof the thatch scarce covers o'er.

And yet for guest he has sufficing store:
His oven is large, his vines make glad the eye,
And in his garden lupines multiply.
'Tis little?—Gallus ne'er has longed for more.

His grove yields fagots through the winter hours,
And shade in summer under leafy bowers,
While autumn brings some passing thrush for prize.

'Tis there, contented with his narrow round,
He ends his days upon his natal ground.
Go, now thou knowest why Gallus is so wise.

THE FLUTE

Lo, evening's here. Some pigeons skyward fly.
O goatherd, nought so soothes love's feverous wound
As pipe well blown, when its appeasing sound
Blends with the sedgy stream's melodial sigh.

In this great plane-tree's shade, where stretched we lie,
The grass is soft. That goat, now rambling round,
Should climb yon rock where tenderest buds abound,
And freely browse beyond her weanling's cry.

With seven unequal stems of hemlock made,
Well joined with wax, my flute, or sharply played
Or grave, weeps, sings, or wails, as I incline.

Come. Learn Silenus' art that knows no death,
And thy love-plaints will, by this pipe divine,
Be driven to flight mid its harmonious breath.

62

THE GOD OF THE GARDENS

To Paul Aréne

ROME AND THE BARBARIANS

THE GOD OF THE GARDENS
I
Olim truncus eram ficulnus
HORACE

COME not! Away! Let not one step be stayed!
Insidious pillager, I fancy you
Would steal the grapes, mad-apples, olives, too,
Which the sun ripens in the orchard's shade.

I watch. A shepherd once with hedge-bill blade
Carved me from fig-tree trunk Ægina knew;
Laugh, but consider how Priapus grew,
And know none can his fierce revenge evade.

Of old, to seamen dear, on galley's beak
With ruddy glow I stood, and joyed to speak
To laughter-sparkling or foam-crested waves;

And now the fruits and herbs I keep watch o'er,
To shield this garden from marauding knaves ...
The smiling Cyclades I'll ne'er see more.

THE GOD OF THE GARDENS

III
Ecce villicus
Venit ...
CATULLUS

Ho, you sly imps! Of dog, of traps, beware!
As guardian here, I would not, for my sake,
Have one pretending garlic bulb to take
Plunder my fruit groves nor my grapevines spare.

Below, the planter mows his field, from where
He spies you; if he comes here, by my stake!
With hard wood wielded by his arm he'll make
Your loins well smoke, whate'er a God may care.

Quick, take the left-hand path, and with it wind
Till at the hedge's end a beech you find;
Then heed the word one slips into your ear:

A negligent Priapus lives near by;
His arbor pillars you can see from here,
Where blushing grapes in shade-wrapped greenery lie.

THE GOD OF THE GARDENS
IV
Mihi Corolla picta vere ponitur
CATULLUS

ENTER. Fresh coated have my pillars been,
And in my arbor, from the sunshine's glare,
The shade is softest. Balm perfumes the air,
And April decks the ground with blossomy sheen.

By turns the seasons crown me: olives green,
Ripe grapes, great golden ears, and flower-cups fair;
While goats their creamy milk still kindly spare,
Which curded in the vat each morn is seen.

The master honors me for service done;
Nor thrush nor thief despoils his vines, and none
Is better guarded in the Roman land.

Sons fair, wife virtuous, the man at home
Each eve from market jingles in his hand
The shining deniers he has brought from Rome.

ROME AND THE BARBARIANS

THE GOD OF THE GARDENS

                  V   *Rigetque dura barba juncta crystallo*
                                        Diversorum poetarum lusus

How cold! The vines with frost are glittering;
The sun I watch for, knowing the time exact
When dawn red tints Soracte's snows. Distract
Is rural God—man's so perverse a thing.

For twenty winters, lonely, shivering,
In this old close I've lived. My beard's compact,
My paint scales off, my shrunken wood is cracked,
And now the worms may come to gnaw and sting.

Why of Penates am I not, or Lar
Domestic even, retouched, from care afar,
With fruits and honey gorged, or wreathed, as they?

In the fore-court the wax ancestors grace
I should grow old, and on their virile day
The children round my neck their bullæ place.

See note p. 172.

70

TRANQUILLUS

C. Plinii Secundi Epist. Lib. I, Ep. XXIV

Suetonius' pleasing country this; and he
Near Tibur raised his humble villa where
Some vine-clad wall the years still kindly spare,
And arcade's ruin wreathed in greenery.

Here, far from Rome, he came each fall to see
The sky's last azure, and from elm-trees' care
To take the plenteous grapes empurpling there.
His life flowed on in calm tranquility.

In this sweet pastoral peace would Claudius bide,
Caligula and Nero; here, with pride,
Vile Messalina in her purple strolled;

And here with pointed stylus he has told,
Scratched in the unpitying wax, of him who tried
In Capri all that's foul when he was old.

See note p. 174.

72

ROME AND THE BARBARIANS

THE TREBIA

Dawn tints the heights on this ill day of need.
The camp has roused. The waters roaring go
Where the Numidian light-horse drink below,
And everywhere the pealing trumpets plead.

For spite of Scipio, of the augurs' rede,
Of wind and rain, the Trebia's swollen flow,
Sempronius Consul, proud new fame to know,
Has bade his lictors with the axe proceed.

The Insubres their burning homes behold,
The horizon reddening with the flames uprolled,
While far resounds the elephant's loud cry.

Beneath the bridge, leaning against an arch,
Deep-musing Hannibal, with triumph high,
Lists to the tramping legions as they march.

ROME AND THE BARBARIANS

AFTER CANNÆ

ONE consul killed; one to Venusia fled,
Or to Liternum; the Aufidus runs o'er
From dead and arms; lightning has struck full sore
The Capitol; the bronze sweats, and the heavens look drea

Vainly the God's feast has the Pontiff spread,
And twice the Sibyl's Oracle did implore,
The grandsire, widow, orphan, weep yet more,
Till Rome in consternation bows her head.

Each evening to the aqueducts they swarm:
Plebs, slaves, the women, children, the deform—
All that the prison or the slum can spew—

To see, on Sabine Mount of blood-hued dyes,
Seated on elephant Gætulian, rise
The one-eyed Chieftain to their anxious view.

See note p. 176.

ROME AND THE BARBARIANS

TO A TRIUMPHER

Illustrious Imperator, thine arch crown
With old chiefs yoked, barbarian warriors' throng,
Bits that to armor and to boats belong,
With beak and stern of ships thine arms struck down.

Whoe'er thou art, from Ancus sprung or clown,
Thy honors, names and lineage, short or long,
In bas-reliefs and frieze engrave them strong,
That future years dim not thy just renown.

Even now Time lifts his fatal arm. Dost hope
To give thy fame's report eternal scope?
Why, let an ivy climb, thy trophy dies;

And on thy blazoned blocks, dispersed and rent,
As choked with grass their glory's ruin lies,
Some Samnite mower will his scythe indent.

ANTONY AND CLEOPATRA

ANTONY AND CLEOPATRA

THE CYDNUS

Beneath triumphal blue, in flaming ray,
The silver trireme tints the dark flood white,
And censers breathe rich perfumes that unite
With rustling silks and flutes' mellifluous play.

Where, at the prow, the spread-hawk holds his way,
Cleopatra forward leans for better sight,
And seems, as stands she in the evening light,
Like some great golden bird in watch for prey.

Now Tarsus sees the warrior captive there:
The dusky Lagian opes, in that charmed air,
Her amber arms with roseate purple dyed;

Nor has she seen anear, as fateful sign,
Shredding the roses on the sombrous tide,
Those twins, Desire and Death, of life divine.

See note p. 176.

80

ANTONY AND CLEOPATRA

On Egypt sleeping in the sultry air
The twain gazed wistful from their terrace high,
Where far they could the Delta's flood descry
Toward Saïs or Bubastis onward fare.

Beneath his thick cuirass he, born to dare,—
A captive now to croon a lullaby,—
Felt on his conquering heart surrendered lie
Her form voluptuous pressed still closelier there.

Turning her pale face mid its locks of brown
To him whose reason perfumes had struck down,
She raised her mouth and luring, lustrous eye;

And bent o'er her the chief could but behold
In her great orbs, starry with dots of gold,
Only unbounded seas where galleys fly.

See note p. 176.

EPIGRAPHIC SONNETS

Bagnères-de-Luchon, Sept. 188...

EPIGRAPHIC SONNETS

ILIXONI
DEO
FAB. FESTA
V. S. L. M.

THE VOW

ISCITTO DEO
HVNNV
VLOHOXIS
FIL.
V. S. L. M.

THE light-haired Gaul, he of Iberian strain,
The brown Garumnus in his paint, of old,
Upon the marble cut by them have told
This water's virtue and its power o'er bane.

The Roman pool and thermæ to ordain
The Emperors at Venasque then made bold,
When Fabia Festa, like the rest controlled,
Gave to the Gods the mallow and vervain.

As when Ilixon and Iscitt were young
The Springs to-day their song to me have sung,
Where the pure air the sulphur fumes still know.

Hence in this vow-made verse 'tis mine to raise,
Like Ulohox's son in bygone days,
A rough-hewn altar to the nymphs below.

See note p. 177.

EPIGRAPHIC SONNETS

THE SPRING

NYMPHIS AVG. SACRVM

In brier and grass the altar buried sleeps,
Where falling drop by drop the nameless spring
Fills the lone vale with plaintive murmuring:
It is the Nymph that o'er Oblivion weeps.

This useless mirror which no wavelet sweeps,
The dove now seldom kisses with her wing,
And but the moon, through dark skies wandering,
Her pallid face alone upon it keeps.

At times a passing herdsman here delays;
He drinks; then pours the drops, his thirst all flown,
From out his hand upon the road's old stone.

In this the ancestral gesture he betrays,
The Roman cippus to his eye unknown
With patera near the libatory vase.

See note p. 177.

EPIGRAPHIC SONNETS

THE BEECH-TREE GOD

FAGO DEO

THE house of the Garumnus glads the ground
Beneath a gnarlèd, mighty beech where wells
A God's pure sap by which the white bark swells.
The mother forest makes his utmost bound;

For by the seasons blest he there has found
Nuts, wood and shade, and creatures that he fells
With bow and spear, or with sly lures compels,
For flesh to eat or fleece to wrap him round.

The years have crowned his toil and made him free;
And on his home-return at eve the Tree
With kindly arms seems proffering welcome's good;

And when death comes to lower his lofty brow,
His grandsons will cut out his coffin's wood
From the sound heart of its supremest bough.

See note p. 177.

EPIGRAPHIC SONNETS

TO THE DIVINE MOUNTAINS

GEMINVS SERVVS
ET PRO SVIS CONSERVIS

BLUE glaciers, peaks of marble, granite, slate,
Moraines whose winds send blighting ruin through
The wheat and rye from Bègle to Néthou;
Lakes, woods of shade and nest, steep crags serrate;

Lone caves, dark vales, where exiles desolate,
Sooner than crouch before the tyrant crew,
Wolf, chamois, eagle, bear, as comrades knew;
Abysses, torrents, cliffs, blest be your state!

From cruel town and prison when he flew,
Geminus, the slave, this cippus gave unto
The Mountains, sacred guards of liberty;

And on these silence-pulsing summits clear,
In this pure, boundless air's immensity,
A freeman's cry still falls upon mine ear.

See note p. 177.

EPIGRAPHIC SONNETS

THE EXILED

MONTIBVS. . .
GARRI DEO. . . .
SABINVLA
V. S. L. M.

IN this wild vale where Cæsar bids thee sigh,
With bended, silvered head too early snowed,
Slowly each eve along the Ardiège road
Thou comest on the moss-grown rock to lie.

Thy youth, thy villa, greet again thine eye,
And Flamen red, as when with train he strode;
And so to ease thy longing's heavy load,
Sad Sabinula, thou regard'st the sky.

Toward seven-pointed Gar with splendors bright,
The tardy eagles hastening to their height
Bear on their wings the dreams that fill thy mind;

And so, without desire or hope, and lost to home,
Thou raisest altars to the Mountains kind,
Whose neighboring Gods now solace thee for Rome.

See note p. 177.

THE MIDDLE AGE AND THE RENAISSANCE

MIDDLE AGE AND RENAISSANCE

A CHURCH WINDOW

THIS window has seen dames and lords of might,
Sparkling with gold, with azure, flame and nacre,
Bow down before the altar of their Maker
The pride of crest and hood to sacred right,

Whene'er to horn's or clarion's sound, with tight
Held sword in hand, gerfalcon or the saker,
Toward plain or wood, Byzantium or Acre,
They started for crusade or herons' flight.

To-day, the seigniors near their chatelaines,
With hound low crouching at their long poulaines,
Upon the marble floor extended lie;

All voiceless, deaf and motionless are they,
Whose eyes of stone look on the window nigh,
Yet cannot see its rose that blooms alway.

MIDDLE AGE AND RENAISSANCE

EPIPHANY

THEN, Balthazar, Melchior, Gaspar—Magian Kings,
With gorgeous vases where enamels glow,
And silver, and by camels followed, go
As in the bodied, old imaginings.

From the far East they bear their offerings
To that divine One born to suage the woe
Of man and beast who suffer here below.
Their robes beflowered a page upbearing brings.

Where Joseph waits them at the stable's door,
With Chieftain's crown they bend the Child before,
Who laughs and eyes them with admiring mien.

So, when Augustus ruled in time of old,
The royal Magians from afar were seen
Presenting precious incense, myrrh, and gold.

MIDDLE AGE AND RENAISSANCE

THE WOOD-WORKER OF NAZARETH

To make a dresser the good master here
Has ceaseless toiled since dawn with weary strain,
Handling by turns the chisel and the plane,
The grating rasp and smoothing polisher.

With pleasure hence he sees, toward eve, draw near
The lengthening shadow of the great platane,
Where blessèd Mary and her mother Saint Anne,
With Jesus nigh them, go for restful cheer.

The parching air stirs not the leaves at all;
And Joseph, sore fatigued, his gouge lets fall,
As with his apron he would dry his face;

While the pure Prentice, in a glory's fold,
Makes alway, in the shop's obscurest place,
Fly from the cutting edge his chips of gold.

MIDDLE AGE AND RENAISSANCE

A MEDAL

RIMINI'S Lord, Vicar and Podestate:—
His hawked profile, clearly or vaguely seen
In tawny glimmer as of day's last sheen,
Lives in this medal de' Pastis did create.

Of all the tyrants whom a people hate,
Count, Duke or Marquis, Prince or Princeling e'en,—
Galeas, Hercules, Can or Ezzelin,—
None can the haughty Malatesta mate.

This one, the best, this Sigismond Pandolf,
Laid waste Romagna, Marches and the Gulf,
A temple built, made love, and sang the while;

And e'en their loveliest lack refinement's crown,
For on the bronze that sees Isotta smile
The Elephant triumphal tramps the primrose down.

MIDDLE AGE AND RENAISSANCE

THE RAPIER

CALIXTUS Pope we on the pommel read.
The keys, tiara, boat and fish-net bear
Their rich reliefs upon the sword's guard where
Emblazoned glows the ox of Borgian breed;

Within the fusil laughs, mid coral seed
By ivy twined, Faun or Priapus fair,
Till raised to splendor by the enamel there,
The rapier's more for wonder than for need.

Antonio Perez de Las Cellas planned
This pastoral staff for the first Borgia's hand,
As though his famous brood he had foretold;

And better far than Ariosto's phrase,
Or Sannazar's, this steel, with hilt of gold,
Pope Alexander and the Prince portrays.

MIDDLE AGE AND RENAISSANCE

AFTER PETRARCH

As you came out of church, with piety
Your noble hands bestowed alms freely where
Within the porch's shade you shone so fair,
The poor all heaven's great riches seemed to see.

I then saluted you most graciously—
Humbly, as suits one in discretion's care;
When, drawing close your robe, with angry air
Your face you shaded as you turned from me.

But Love that will the most rebellious rule,
Would not consent, less kind than beautiful,
That mercy should let pity pass me by;

And in your veiling you were then so slow,
The umbrageous lashes of your beaming eye
Throbbed like dark leafage in the starlight's glow.

MIDDLE AGE AND RENAISSANCE

ON THE BOOK OF LOVES OF PIERRE DE RONSARD

In Bourgueil Gardens more than one of yore
Engraved upon the bark names fondly sweet,
And many a heart 'neath Louvre's gold ceilings beat,
At flash of smile, with pride which thrilled to soar.

What matters it?—their joy or grief is o'er;
They lie in stillness where four oak boards meet
Beneath the sighing grass, with none to greet
Their voiceless dust that feeds oblivion's shore.

All die. Mary, Helen, Cassandra bold,
Your lovely forms would be but ashes cold,
—Nor rose nor lily sees the morrow's land—

Had Ronsard by the Seine or Loire not wove
For brows of yours, with an immortal hand,
Fame's laurel leaf with myrtle leaf of Love.

MIDDLE AGE AND RENAISSANCE

THE BEAUTIFUL VIOLE

TO HENRY CROS

BY JOACHIM DU BELLAY

A vous trouppe légère
Qui d'aile passagère
Par le monde volez . . .

UPON the balcony, where her longing eyes
The road to far-off Italy can trace,
'Neath a pale olive branch she bows her face.
The violet blooms to-day, to-morrow dies.

Her viol then with fragile hand she tries,
That soothes her solitude and saddened case,
And dreams of him whose heedless footsteps pace
The dust wherein Rome's fallen grandeur lies.

The soul of her he called his Angevine sweet
Bids each vibrating string divinely beat,
Whene'er her troubled heart feels love's sharp pain;

And on the winds her notes far distant run,

MIDDLE AGE AND RENAISSANCE

AN EPITAPH

After the Verses of Henry III

O PASSER, Hyacinthe lies hallowed here,
Who, Lord of Maugiron was, now cold as stone—
God rest the soul, and all the sins condone,
Of him who fell unshaken with a fear.

None, not e'en Quélus decked with pearl-gemmed gear,
In plaited ruff or plumed cap princelier shone,
And so thou seest this mournful marble own
A branch of jacinth cut by Myron's peer.

King Henry kissed and clipped him and his shroud
Put on; then willed that to Saint-Germain proud
Be borne his pale, cold form of matchless grace;

And that such grief as his might never die,
He raised this emblem in this sacred place—
Sad, sweet memorial of Apollo's sigh.

MIDDLE AGE AND RENAISSANCE

GILDED VELLUM

T HE gold, old Master Binder, thou didst chase
On the book's back and in the edge's grain,
Despite the irons pushed with free-hand main,
In vivid, brilliant hue no more we trace.

The figures which so deftly interlace
Grow daily on the fine, white skin less plain;
And scarce we see the ivy thou didst train
To wind in beauty o'er the cover's space.

But this translucent, supple ivory,
Marguerite, Marie — Diane, it e'en may be,
With loving fingers have of old caressed;

And this paled vellum Clovis Eve gilt seems
To evoke, I know not by what charm possessed,
Their perfume's spirit and shadow of their dreams.

MIDDLE AGE AND RENAISSANCE

THE DOGARESSA

Upon the marble porticos all these
Great lords converse who live through Titian's lore,
And whose rich collars, weighing marc or more,
Enhance their red dalmatic draperies.

With eyes where shine patrician dignities,
The old lagoons they look serenely o'er,
Beneath clear skies of Venice, to the shore
And sparkling azure of the Adrian seas.

And while in brilliant throng full many a Knight
Trails gold and purple by the stairs of white,
Bathed in cerulean sheen all joys constrain;

Indolent, superb, a Dame, retired in shade,
Turning half round in billows of brocade,
Smiles at the negro boy who bears her train.

MIDDLE AGE AND RENAISSANCE

ON THE OLD BRIDGE

Antonio di Sandro orefice

THE Master Goldsmith has, since matins, where
Beneath his pencils the enamel flowed,
On clasp or on nielloed pax bestowed
Latin devices in resplendence rare.

Upon the Bridge, where bells made glad the air,
Camail and frock were by the cape elbowed;
And when the heaven like some church window glowed,
The lovely Florentines were haloed there.

And quick beguiled by dream that passion knows,
The pensive prentices forgot to close
On ring's chaton the lovers' hands in plight;

MIDDLE AGE AND RENAISSANCE

THE OLD GOLDSMITH

THAN any Master the maitrise can blaze,
E'en Ruyz, Arphé, Ximeniz, Becerrill,
All gems I've deftlier set, and with more skill
Have wrought the frieze and handle of the vase.

In silver, on the enamel's irised glaze,
I've carved and painted, to my soul's worst ill,
Shame, not the Rood, and saint upon the grill,
But Bacchus drunk or Danaë's amaze.

The rapier's iron I've damaskeened full well,
And, for vain boastings of these works of hell,
Adventured the eternal part of me;

And now, as fast my years toward evening fly,
O would, as did Fray Juan de Segovie,
While chasing gold of monstrance I might die.

MIDDLE AGE AND RENAISSANCE

THE SWORD

TRUST me, my pious child, take the old road:
This sword, with straight cross-guards in twist aright,
Used by an ardent gentleman of might,
Is lighter than a Romish ritual's load.

Take it. The Hercules thy touch has glowed,
Its gold by thy grandsires' use kept bright,
Now swells beneath its surface splendor-dight
The beauteous, iron muscles of a God.

Try it. The supple steel a bouquet shows
Of sparks. The solid blade is one of those
To send a prideful shiver through the breast;

Bearing, in hollow of its brilliant gorge,
Like noble Dame a gem, the stamp impressed
Of Julian del Rey, prince of the forge.

MIDDLE AGE AND RENAISSANCE

TO CLAUDIUS POPELIN

On fragile glass, within the lead's embrace,
Old Masters painted lords of high degree
Turning their chaperons full piously,
And bowed in prayer, as though of bourgeois race.

The breviary's page some loved to grace
With saints and ornaments a joy to see,
Or made to glow, by pliant touch and free,
With arabesques the ewer's bellied space.

To-day, Claudius, their rival and their son,
Reviving in himself their works sublime,
On lasting metal has his triumphs won;

And hence, beneath the enamel of my rhyme,
I would keep green upon his brow alway,
For future ages, the heroic Bay.

MIDDLE AGE AND RENAISSANCE

ENAMEL

Now take thy lamp; the oven for plaque doth glow;
Model paillon where irised colors run,
And fix with fire in the pigment dun
The sparkling powder which thy pencils know.

Wilt thou the bay or myrtle wreath bestow
On thinker, hero, prince, or love's dear one?
By what God wilt, on sky unlit by sun,
The glaucous sea-horse or scaled hydra show?

No. Rather let a sapphire orb reveal
From Ophir's warrior race some proud profile —
Thalestris, Bradamant, Penthesilea.

And that her beauty may be still more fell,
Casque her blonde locks with wingèd beast, and be a
Gold gorgon on her bosom's lovely swell.

MIDDLE AGE AND RENAISSANCE

DREAMS OF ENAMEL

In the dark chamber roars the athanor,
Whose brick-cased fire, in ardent, glowing state,
Breathes on the copper till it there will mate
With gold's own splendor from enamel's store.

Beneath my brushes are born, live, run and soar
Mythology's rare race: Bacchus' wild fête,
Chimæra, Centaurs, Sphinx, and Pan the great,
With Gorgon, Pegasus and Chrysaor.

Shall I now paint Achilles weeping near
Penthesilea? Orpheus' banished dear
For whom the infernal gate will ne'er relent?

Hercules confounding the Avernian hound,
Or Virgin at the cavern's outer bound
With writhing body which the Dragons scent?

THE CONQUERORS

THE CONQUERORS

As falcons from their native eyrie soar,
So, tired of woes long borne with haughty air,
Bold-hearted men from Palos and Moguer
Went forth with daring dreams mad to the core.

They longed to seize the fabled metal store
Cipango's mines in rich perfection bear,
And favoring breezes bade their brave prows dare
The dim, mysterious occidental shore.

At eve, as Hope unveiled each epic view,
The tropic sea's bright phosphorescent blue
Bewitched their slumbers with mirage of gold;

Or from the foredeck of their caravels
On alien skies they wondered to behold
Strange stars new risen from ocean's glowing wells.

See note p. 182.

THE CONQUERORS

YOUTH

J UAN Ponce de Leon, by the Devil led,
With years weighed down, and crammed with antique lore
Seeing age blanch his scanty hair still more,
The far seas scoured to find Health's Fountainhead.

By vain dream haunted his Armada sped
Three years the glaucous wildness to explore,
Till through the fog of the Bermudan shore
Loomed Florida whose skies enchantment shed.

Then the Conquistador his madness blessed,
And with enfeebled hand his pennon pressed
In that bright earth which opened for his tomb.

Old man, most happy thou: thy fortune sooth
To deathlike, but thy dream bears beauty's bloom

THE CONQUERORS

THE TOMB OF THE CONQUEROR

Where the catalpa's arches cast their shade,
Where the black tulip tree white-petaled blows,
He finds not in the fatal earth repose;
Through vanquished Florida he passed unstayed.

For such as he no paltry tomb be made;
For shroud, the Western India's conqueror shows
The Mississippi which above him flows.
Nor Redskins nor gray bears his rest invade.

He sleeps where virgin waters carved his couch;
What matters monument, the taper's vouch,
The psalm, the chapel and the offering?

Since northen winds, amid the cypress' sighs,
Eternal supplications weep and sing
O'er the Great River where de Soto lies.

THE CONQUERORS

IN THE TIME OF CHARLES THE FIFTH EMPEROR

WE place him with the famed ones passed away,
For his adventurous keel the first was seen
To thread the island Gardens of the Queen,
Where breezes made of perfumes ever play.

Far more than years, the surge and biting spray,
Infuriate storms, and long, long calms between,
Love of the mermaid and the fright, I ween,
Blanched his brown hair and turned his beard to gray.

Through him Castile led Triumph o'er the seas,
For his fleet crowned her that unrivaled one
Whose boundless empire saw no setting sun.

Prince of all pilots, Bartolomé Ruis,
Who, on the royal arms, still lustrous told,
Bears anchor sable with its chain of gold.

THE ANCESTOR

TO CLAUDIUS POPELIN

GLORY has cut its noble furrows o'er
This Cavalier's stern face, whose dauntless air
Proclaims he yielded not when the fierce glare
Of war and torrid sun beat on him sore.

In every place the sacred Cross he bore—
Sierras, Terra Firma, Islands fair;
The Andes scaled; then led his pennon where
The Gulf's waves whiten the Floridian shore.

Thy pencils, Claudius, bid his kin behold,
In his bronze mail splendid with foliage scrolled,
In life again their moody, proud grandsire;

His glowering eye still searching as of old,
In the enamel's heaven of lustrous fire,
For dazzling glories of Castile of Gold.

See note p. 183.

THE CONQUERORS

TO A FOUNDER OF A CITY

Weary with seeking Ophir's shadowy strand
Thou foundedst, on this gulf's enchanting shore
Which thou the royal standard raisedst o'er
A modern Carthage for the fabled land.

Thou wouldst not have thy name by men unscanned,
And thoughtst to bind it fast forevermore
To this thy City's mortar mixed with gore;
But thy hope, Soldier, rested on the sand.

For Cartagena sees, all choked her breath,
From her dark palaces, thy wall meet death
In ocean's feverous, unrelenting stream;

And for thy crest alone, O Conqueror bold,
As proof heraldic of thy splendid dream,
A silver city glows 'neath palm of gold.

THE CONQUERORS

TO THE SAME

THEIR Inca, Aztec, Yaquis, let them flaunt;
Their Andes, forest, river or their plain—
These men of whom no marks or proofs remain
Save titled show of Marquis or of Count.

But thou didst found—boast that my race can vaunt—
A modern Carthage in the Carib main,
And Magdalena even to Darien
Where flows Atrato, saw the Cross high mount.

Upon thine isle, where waves their breakers hurl,
Despite the centuries' storms and man's mad raids,
Her forts and convents still their stoutness hold;

Hence thy last sons, with trefoil, ache or pearl,
Crest not their scutcheon, but with palm that shades
A silver city with its plume of gold.

THE CONQUERORS

TO A DEAD CITY

Cartagena de Indias
1533-1585-1697

City deject, the Queen whom seas obeyed!—
Unhindered now the shark pursues its prey,
And where the giant galleons proudly lay
Nought but some wandering cloud now casts a shade.

Since Drake's fell heretics' rapacious raid
Thy lonely walls have mouldered in decay,
And, like some collar gloomed by pearls of gray,
Show gaping holes by Pointis' cannon made.

Between the burning sky and foamy sea,
Amid the sun's noontide monotony,
Thou dream'st, O Warrior, of thy conquering men;

And in the languorous evenings warm and calm,
Cradling thy glory lost, O City, then
Thou sleep'st to long-drawn rustling of the palm.

See note p. 183.

THE ORIENT AND THE TROPICS

VISION OF KHEM

I

M<small>ID</small>-DAY. The air burns; beneath the blazing sky
The languid river rolls in leaden flight;
The blinding zenith darts its arrowy light,
And on all Egypt glares Phra's pitiless eye.

The sphinxes with undrooping eyelids lie
Lapped in the scorching sand, with tranquil sight,
Mysterious, changeless, fixed upon the white
Needles of stone upreared so proudly high.

Nought stains or specks the heaven serene and clear
Save the far vultures in unending sweep;
The boundless flame lulls man and beast to sleep;

The parched soil crackles, and Anubis here,
Amid these joys of heat immobile one,
With brazen throat in silence bays the sun.

ORIENT AND TROPICS

VISION OF KHEM
II

THE moon on Nilus sheds resplendent light;
And see, the old death-city stirs amain,
Where kings their hieratic pose maintain
In bandelette and funeral coating dight.

Unnumbered as in days of Ramses' might
The hosts, all noiseless forming mystic train,
(A multitude granitic dreams enchain)
With stately, ordered ranks, march in the night.

They leave the hieroglyphic walls' array
Behind the Bari, which the priests convey,
Of Ammon-Ra, the sun's almighty head;

And sphinxes, and the rams with disk of red,
Uprise at once in wild amaze as they
Break with a start from their eternal bed.

See note p. 184.

ORIENT AND TROPICS

VISION OF KHEM
III

And the crowd grows, increasing more and more:
The dead come forth from hypogeum's night,
And from cartouche the sacred hawks in flight
Mid the great host in freedom proudly soar.

Beasts, peoples, kings, they go. Fierce foreheads o'er,
The gold uræus curls with sparkling light,
But thick bitumen seals their thin lips tight.
At head, the Gods: Hor, Knoum, Ptah, Neith, Hathor;

Next, those whom Ibis-headed Thoth controls,
In shenti robed and crowned with pshent all decked
With lotus blue. The pomp triumphant rolls

Amid the dreadful gloom of temples wrecked,
While the cold pavements wrapped in moonlit air
Show giant shadows strangely lengthened there.

ORIENT AND TROPICS

THE PRISONER

TO GÉRÔME

MUEZZINS' calls have ceased. The greenish sky
Is fringed with gold and purple in the West;
The crocodile now seeks the mud for rest,
And hushed to stillness is the Flood's last cry.

On crossed legs, smoker-wise, with dreamy eye,
The Chief sits mute, by haschisch fumes oppressed,
While on the gangia's rowing bench with zest
Their bending oars two naked negroes ply.

Jocund and jeering, in the stern-sheets where
He scrapes harsh guzla to a savage air,
An Arnaut lolls with brutal look and vile;

For fettered to the boat and bleeding thence,
An old sheik views with grave and stupid sense
The minarets that tremble in the Nile.

ORIENT AND TROPICS

THE SAMURAI

This was a man with two swords

SHE wakes the biwa's softest melodies,
As through the latticed bamboo she espies
The conquering one for whom her love-dream sighs
Advance amid the seashore's fulgencies.

'Tis he, with swords' and fan's rich braveries.
His tasseled girdle steeped in scarlet dyes
Cuts his dark mail, and on his shoulders rise
Hizen's or Togukawa's blazonries.

This handsome warrior in his dress of plate,
Of brilliant lacquers, bronze and silk, would mate
Some black crustacean, gigantesque, vermeil.

He sees her;—and he smiles behind his mask,
While his more rapid pace makes brighter still
The two gold horns that tremble on his casque.

See note p. 187.

ORIENT AND TROPICS

THE DAIMIO

Morning of battle

STUNG by the war-whip, that four pompons has,
The martial, neighing stallion prances high,
And with the clank of sabre rattlings fly
From metal-plated skirt and bronze cuirass.

The Chief, in lacquer dressed, crepon and brass,
Frees his smooth face from bearded mask, to eye
Nippon's dawn smiling in the roseate sky
Upon the far volcano's snow-crowned mass.

But in the gold-hued east the star's bright ray,
Lighting in glory this disastrous day,
He sees above the sea resplendent glow;

To shield his eyes that would no terror shun,
His iron fan he opens with a blow,
Where burns its satin with a crimson sun.

See note p. 187.

ORIENT AND TROPICS

FLOWERS OF FIRE

In ages past, since Chaos' mighty throes,
This crater's pit its flaming brood unchained,
Till grandly lone its fiery plume attained
A loftier height than Chimborazo knows.

Yet Silence here with muffled footstep goes,
The bird now slakes his thirst where cinders rained,
While earth's congealed blood, lava, has constrained
The soil to deep, inviolate repose.

Yet,—act supreme of fire in time of old,—
Within the crater's mouth forever cold,
Making the comminuted rocks to glow,

Like peal of thunder in the silence rolled,
Standing in pollen dust of powdered gold,
The flame-born cactus opes its gorgeous blow.

ORIENT AND TROPICS

THE CENTURY FLOWER

On topmost point of calcined rocky steeps,
Where the volcanic flux dried up of yore,
The seed which winds from Huallatiri bore
Sprout, and the holding plant in frailness creeps.

It grows. Its roots dip down to darkness' deeps,
And light gives nourishment from out its store,
Till a century's suns have ripened more and more
The huge bud whose bent stalk it proudly keeps.

At last, in air that burns it as of old,
With giant pistil raised, it bursts, when lo!
The stamen darts afar the pollen's gold;

And the grand aloe, with its scarlet blow,
That vainly dreamed of Hymen's love-lit way
One hundred years, now blooms but for a day.

See note p. 187.

ORIENT AND TROPICS

THE CORAL REEF

The sun beneath the wave, like strange dawn shown,
Illumes the unbounded coral forest trees,
Where mix in tepid basins of the seas
The living plants with creatures flower-like blown.

And those that salt's or iodine's tints have known—
Moss, algæ, urchins and anemones—
Cover, with purple, sumptuous traceries,
The madrepore's vermiculated stone.

A monstrous fish, whose iridescence dims
Enamel's sheen, across the branches swims.
In lucid shade he indolently preys;

And, sudden, from his fin of flaming hue
A shiver, through the immobile, crystal-blue,
Of emerald, gold and nacre swiftly plays.

NATURE AND DREAM

NATURE AND DREAM

THE ANTIQUE MEDAL

ÆTNA still ripes the colors of the vine,
That warmed with its antique Erigone
Theocritus' glad heart; but now not he,
Of those his verse embalmed, could find one sign.

Losing the pure from her profile divine,
Arethusa, who by turns was bond and free,
Mixed in her Grecian blood whate'er could be
Of Saracen rage with pride of Anjou's line.

Time flies. All die. Even marble feels death's dews.
Agrigentum's but a shade, while Syracuse
Sleeps under shroud of her indulgent sky;

And but hard metal fashioning love displayed
In silver medals keeps in bloom the high,
Immortal beauty of Sicilian maid.

NATURE AND DREAM

THE FUNERAL

WHEN ancient warriors Hades made its own,
Their sacred image Greece was wont to bear
To Phocis' lustrous fanes as Pytho there,
Rock-bound and lightning-girdled, ruled alone.

Whereat their Shades, when night in glory shone
On desert gulfs and isles all brightly fair,
Heard, from the headlands' height in radiant air,
Famed Salamis above their tombs intone.

But I, when old, in lengthening grief shall die,
And then nailed down in narrow coffin lie,
The earth's and tapers' cost, with priest's fee, paid;

And yet, in many a dream my soul aspires
To sink into the sun, even as the sires,
Still young and wept by hero and by maid.

See note p. 189.

NATURE AND DREAM

THE VINTAGE

The wearied vintagers their tasks resign
With voices ringing in eve's tremulous air,
And as the women toward the wine-press fare,
They sing mid raillery and gesturing sign.

All white with flying swans the skies now shine,
As Naxos saw, with fume like censers bear,
When at the orgies sat the Cretan where
The Tamer reveled in the gladdening wine.

But Dionysus, with his thyrsus bright,
Who beasts and Gods made subject to his might,
Girds the wreathed yoke on panther nevermore;

Yet Autumn, daughter of the Sun, still twines
In dark and golden tresses, as of yore,
The sanguine leaves and branches of the vines.

SIESTA

No sound of insect or marauding bee;
All sleep in woods that droop beneath the sun,
Whose light, through foliage strained, its way has won
To emerald moss with bosom velvety.

Piercing the dusky dome bright Noon roams free,
And o'er my lashes half with sleep foredone
Bids myriad glints and gleamings furtive run,
That lace the shade with vermeil tracery.

Toward fiery gauze the rays inweave now hies
The fragile swarm of gorgeous butterflies,
Mad with sap's perfume and the luminous beams;

And tremulous fingers on each thread I set,
As in gold meshes of this tenuous net,
Hunter of harmonies, I prison my dreams.

THE SEA OF BRITTANY

To Emmanuel Lansyer

NATURE AND DREAM

A PAINTER

HE knows the ancient, pensive race of dry
And flinty Breton soil—unvaried plain
Of rose and gray, where yew and ivy reign
O'er crumbling manors which beneath them lie.

From wind-swept slopes of writhing beech his eye
Has joyed to see mid autumn's boisterous train
The red sun sink beneath the foamy main,
His lips all salt with spray from reefs dashed high.

He paints the ocean, splendorous, vast and sad,
With cloud in amethystine beauty clad,
In frothy emerald and calm sapphire;

He fixes fast the things which else would fly,
And on his narrow canvas makes respire,
In the sand's mirror, the occidental sky.

NATURE AND DREAM

BRITTANY

THAT joyous blood thy fretful mood may quell,
Thy lungs should deeply drink the Atlantic air
Perfumed with wrack the sea delights to bear.
Arvor has capes the surge besprinkles well,

And furze and heather all their glories tell.
The demons', dwarfs' and clans' own land so fair,
Friend, on the mountain's granite guard with care—
Immobile man near thing immutable.

Come. Everywhere on moors about Arès
Mounts toward heaven—cypress no hand can slay—
The menhir's column raised above the Brave;

And Ocean, that beds with algæ's golden store
Voluptuous Is and mighty Occismor,
Will soothe thy sadness with his cradling wave.

See note p. 189.

NATURE AND DREAM

A FLOWERY SEA

O'ER pied plateau the wave-swept harvest flows,
Rolls, undulates and breaks, with wind rocked high,
While yon dark harrow, profiled on the sky,
Seems like some vessel in the tempest's throes.

With blue, cerulean, violet or rose,
Or fleecy white from sheep the ebb makes fly,
The sea, far as the West's empurpling dye,
Like boundless meadow verdurously glows.

The gulls, that watch the tide with eager care,
On whirling wing with screams of joy fly where
The ripened grain in golden billow lies;

While from the land a breeze of sweets possessed
Disperses o'er the ocean's flowery breast
In wingèd rapture swarms of butterflies.

See note p. 190.

SUNSET

The blossomed furze — gem of the granite's crest —
Gilds all the height the sun's last glories fill,
And far below, with foam refulgent still,
Unbounded spreads great ocean's heaving breast.

Silence and Night are at my feet. The nest
Is hushed; the smoking thatch folds man from ill;
And but the Angelus, with melodious thrill,
Lifts its calm voice amid the sea's unrest.

Then, as from bottom of abyss, there rise
From trails, ravines and moors the distant cries
Of tardy herdsmen who their kine reclaim.

In deepening shade the whole horizon lies,
And the dying sun upon the rich, sad skies
Shuts the gold branches of his fan of flame.

NATURE AND DREAM

STAR OF THE SEA

WITH linen coifs, arms crossed on breast, and dight
In thin percale, or in wool's coarse array,
The kneeling women on the quay survey
The Isle of Batz which looms all foamy white.

Their fathers, husbands, lovers, sons, unite
With Paimpol's, Audierne's, and Cancale's, away
For the far North to sail. How many may,
Of these bold fishers, see no more home's light!

Above the noise of ocean and of shore
The plaintive chant ascends as they implore
The Holy Star—sailor's last hope in ill;

While the Angelus, each face in prayerful wise,
From Roscoff's towers to those of Sybiril,
In the pale, roseate heavens, floats, throbs, and dies.

NATURE AND DREAM

THE BATH

THE man and beast, like antique monster, free,
Reinless and nude, the sea have entered in
Mid the gold mist of pungent pulverin—
Athletic group on sky's refulgency.

The savage horse, and tamer rude as he,
Breathe the brine's fragrance deep their lungs within,
As mad with joy they feel upon their skin
The Atlantic's billows beating icily.

The surge swells, runs, wall-like is piled,
Then breaks. They cry. His tail the stallion plies
Until the wave in jets transplendent flies;

And with disheveled locks and aspect wild
Their smoking, heaving breasts they well oppose
Against the foam-crowned breakers' lashing blows.

NATURE AND DREAM

CELESTIAL BLAZON

I'VE seen upon the azure of the West
The clouds all silvery, purple, coppery, make
Great forms before the dazzled vision take
The shape of blazon splendently impressed.

An heraldic beast, for bearers or for crest,
Alerion, leopard, unicorn or snake—
Huge captive ones whose chains a gust might break—
Uprears its figure and outswells its breast.

In those strange combats in the vast of space
Of evil seraphs with the archangel race
A heavenly Baron must have won this shield—

Michael or George, perchance; 'tis blazed, I ween,
Like theirs who made Constantinople yield:
The sun, a gold bezant, on sea of green.

NATURE AND DREAM

ARMOR

For guide to Raz a shepherd at Trogor,
Haired like Evhage of old, took me in care;
And then we trod, breathing its spicy air,
The Cymric land with golden broom grown o'er.

The West grew red, and still we walked yet more,
Till to my face the brine its breath did bear;
When cried the man, stretching his long arm where
The landscape lay beyond: Sell euz armor!

And o'er the heather's rose the ocean was seen,
Which, splendent, monstrous, waters with the green
Salt of its waves the cape's granitic breast;

And then my heart, before the horizon's void,
As evening's vasty shade drew toward the West,
The rapture-thrill of space and winds enjoyed.

See note p. 190.

NATURE AND DREAM

A RISING SEA

THE sun a beacon seems with fixed, white light.
From Raz far as Penmarch the coast's in fume,
And only wind-blown gulls with ruffled plume
Through the mad tempest whirl in aimless flight.

With ceaseless roll and fierce, impetuous might
The glaucous waves, beneath their mane of spume
Dispersing clouds of mist to thunderous boom,
The distant, streaming reefs with plumes bedight.

And so the billows of my thought have course—
Spent hopes and dreams, regrets for wasted force,
With nothing left but memory mocking me.

Ocean has spoken in fraternal strain,
For that same clamor which impels the sea
Mounts to the Gods from man, eternal, vain.

See note p. 190.

NATURE AND DREAM

A SEA BREEZE

THE winter has deflowered garden and heath;
Nought lives; and on the rock's unchanging gray,
Where the Atlantic's endless billows play,
The last pistil to petal clings in death.

Yet, what rare scents this sea breeze furnisheth
I know not — grateful, warm effluvia they
That bid my heart to mad delight give way;
Whence comes this strangely odoriferous breath?

Ah, now I know! — 'tis from the far-off West,
Where the Antilles swoon in languorous rest
Beneath the torrid occidental heat;

And from this reef, by Cymric billows rolled,
I've breathed, in winds my natal air made sweet,
America's dear flowers I loved of old.

NATURE AND DREAM

THE SHELL

IN what cold seas, under what winters' reign,
—Who knows, or can know, nacreous, fragile Shell!—
Hast thou mid current, wave and tidal swell,
In shallows and abysses restless lain?

To-day, beneath the sky, far from the main,
Thou hast in golden sands thy bed made well;
But vain thy hope, for still within thy cell
Despairing sounds great ocean's mournful strain.

My soul a prison all sonorous lies,
Where, as of old, complaining tears and sighs
With sad refrain make clamor as in thee;

So from the heart-depths She alone can fill,
Dull, slow, unfeeling, yet eternal still,
The far, tumultuous murmur moans in me.

NATURE AND DREAM

THE BED

WHETHER with serge becurtained or brocade,
Sad as a tomb or joyous as a nest,
'Tis there we mate, are born, lie peace-possessed,
Child, spouse, old man, old woman, wife or maid.

In glad or sad, with holy water sprayed
Under black crucifix or branch that's blest,
All there begins, all there meets final rest,
From life's first light to death's eternal shade.

Rude, humble and closed, or proud with canopy
Whose gorgeous colors blaze triumphantly,
Of cypress's, or oak's, or maple's mould,

Blest he who sleeps, his cares all laid aside,
In that paternal, massive bed of old,
Where all his own were born and all have died.

NATURE AND DREAM

THE EAGLE'S DEATH

Above the sempiternal snow aspires
The vast-winged eagle still to loftier air,
That nearer to the sun, in blue more fair,
He may refresh his sight's undaunted ires.

He rises. Sparks in torrents he inspires.
Still up, in proud, calm flight, he glories where
The tempest draws fell lightnings to its lair;
Whereat his wings are smit by their fierce fires.

With scream, and in the storm-cloud whirling, he,
Sublimely tasting the flame's withering kiss,
Deep plunges to the fulgurant abyss.

Blest he who, thrilled by Fame or Liberty,
In strength's full pride and dream's enrapturing bliss
Dies such heroic, dazzling death as this.

NATURE AND DREAM

MORE BEYOND

MAN has o'ercome the lion's burning zone,
As that of venoms and of reptiles' bale,
And vexed the ocean where the nautili sail
The track which galleons blazoned as their own.

But farther than Spitzbergen's breast of stone,
Than whirlpools dire, or snows that never fail,
The warm, free polar waves the isles assail
Where flag of mariner has never flown.

Depart! The insuperable ice I'll dare,
For my stout spirit would no longer bear
The fame that wreathes the Conquerors of Gold.

I go, to mount the utmost promontory,
And feel the sea, that silences enfold,
Caress my pride with whispered hope of glory.

NATURE AND DREAM

THE LIFE OF THE DEAD

TO THE POET ARMAND SILVESTRE

WHEN over us the cross its shadow throws,
Our frames enshrouded in the mould of night,
Thou wilt reflower in the lily white,
And from my flesh be born the ensanguined rose.

And Death divine thy verse in music knows,
With silence and oblivion to his flight,
Will bear us, cradled in serene delight,
Through charmèd ways that strange new stars disclose.

And mounting to the Sun our spirits twain,
Absorbed and melted in his depths, will gain
The tranquil raptures of unceasing fire;

While friend and poet, by Fame's pure chrism blest,
Will find eternity of life where rest
The immortal Shades made kindred by the Lyre.

NATURE AND DREAM

TO THE TRAGEDIAN
E. ROSSI
AFTER A RECITATION FROM DANTE

I'VE seen thee, Rossi, robed in black, give fair
Ophelia's tender heart thy rending blow,
And, tiger mad with love and phrensied woe,
Read in the handkerchief thy soul's despair.

Macbeth and Lear I've seen, and wept whene'er
I saw thee, who lov'st old Italia so,
Kiss Juliet in her nuptial tomb laid low;
Yet once beyond all these I found thee dare.

For mine the horror and the joy sublime
Of then first listening to the triple rhyme
Sound in thy golden voice its iron swell;

And, lit by flames of the infernal shore,
I saw—and shuddered to my being's core—
The living Dante chant his song of Hell.

NATURE AND DREAM

MICHELANGELO

Haunted he was by torments tragical,
When in the Sistine where no fête he knew,
Lonely, his Sibyls and his Prophets grew,
And his Last Judgment on the sombrous wall.

He heard the tear-drops unremitting fall,—
Titan whose wish to highest summits flew,—
Where Country, Glory, Love, their failures rue;
And deemed that dreams are false, that death wins all.

And so, these Giants, bloodless, weary grown,
These Slaves bound ever to the unyielding stone,
How strangely twisted at his sovran will;

While in the icy-hearted marbles where
His great soul seethes, how runs with vibrant thrill
The passion of a God imprisoned there.

NATURE AND DREAM

ON A BROKEN MARBLE

'Twas pious, O moss, to close those eyes of thine;
For from this wasted wood has fled and gone
The Virgin who the milk and wine poured on
The earth to that fair name which marked the line.

Viburnum, hops and ivy this divine
Ruin enfold—unknowing if 'twas Faun,
Pan, Hermes or Silvanus;—and upon
Its scarred, maimed front their verdurous tendrils twine.

See! The slant ray, caressful as of old,
In its flat face has set two orbs of gold;
As though from lip the vines with laughter run;

And, magic spell, the breeze around it blown,
The leaves, the wavering shadows, and the sun,
Have made a living God of this wrecked stone.

See note p. 191.

HEREDIA DEAD

October 3, 1905

*Vainly you'll call importunate and long
On him to add fresh jewels to his store,
For muse-beloved he dwells forevermore
With all the crowned ones of his lofty song;*

*And in the midst of that imperial throng,
Now newly splendored by his sonnet-lore,
Fame gently seats him, and delights to score
Her beadroll with his name in letters strong:*

*For though he felt not passion's noblest ire
That bears the uttered thought on wings of fire,
Nor made his numbers all the vastness sweep,*

*Yet he was Art's and drank of her desire,
Until Imagination, true and deep,
Burst into beauty on his flawless lyre.*

See note p. 192.

NEMEA (page 9).

The slaying of the Nemean Lion by Hercules is told by Theocritus in wonderfully graphic fashion in his twenty-fifth Idyl. In James Henry Hallard's translation of the Idyls into English will be found a rendering of this Idyl in the hexameters of the original. Andrew Lang has rendered the Idyls into English prose.

CENTAURS AND LAPITHÆ (page 13).

The combat compacted into this sonnet is related in Book XII of Ovid's Metamorphoses and has been rendered into English blank verse by Henry King.

THE AWAKENING OF A GOD (page 30).

Mysterious Spouse by whom the myrrh's bedewed.

Adonis "was said to have been born from a myrrh-tree, the bark of which bursting, after a ten months' gestation, allowed the lovely infant to come forth. According to some, a boar rent the bark with his tusk and so opened a passage for the babe."—Frazer's "Golden Bough," p. 281.

Of the annual celebration by the Syrians and other peoples of the death and resurrection of Adonis, see Frazer's book as above, pp. 276-296.

THE MAGICIAN (page 31).

The late Dr. Jacob Cooper, of Rutgers College, New Jersey, pointed out to me (using now his words) the following:

"In an unknown Greek author, believed to be Aelian, and quoted in defining a word by Suidas in his Greek

Lexicon—in Greek—we have an account of a young woman who was betrothed, under the most solemn circumstances, in the presence and by the authority of the Divinity of the Cabiri. (Betrothals were a part of the duties of these mysterious Divinities, as is shown by a well-known case, viz., of Olympias and Philip, the parents of Alexander the Great.) This damsel, after the solemn betrothal, was deserted by her affianced husband. She, then, as I quote from Suidas's Lexicon, translating the passage:

'Beseeches the Cabiri to avenge her, and follow up (i. e., to pursue to destruction) the perjurer. This is undoubtedly the love-lorn damsel who is the "Magicienne" of your French poet.'

"The Eumolpidai were a priestly family, deriving their origin from a Pelasgian Thracian named Eumolpus—the one with a good voice or melody. They were clothed with long, purple robes which they shook against the threshold of those they cursed. This was a significant action among all ancient peoples—*vide* Nehemiah, Chap. V, v. 13—and is so among orientals to this day."

MARSYAS (page 33).

Thy natal pines that raptured heard thy strains
Burnt not thy flesh, O thou to woes decreed!
Thy bones are shattered, and thy blood-drops feed
The flood the Phrygian Mount pours toward the plains.

That is, not only did Marsyas not have his funeral pyre made of the wood furnished by the pines that saw his birth, and under whose branches he had fluted, but his body was so treated as to frustrate any attempt at sepulture of it. Nothing seems to have been more abhorrent to the Greek mind than the thought of the non-burial, without appropriate rites, of the human body or of its ashes. And this thought was so predominant as to impel the Greeks to inter even the bodies of their enemies slain in battle. Jebbs says, in the Introduction to his translation of the Antigone of Sophocles, that "The Spartan Lysander omitted to bury the Athenians who fell at Ægospotami; and that omission was remembered centuries later, as an indelible stigma upon his name."

And so it was, that the Athenian Generals who had so decisively defeated the Spartans in the great naval battle of the Arginusæ, were treated with ignominy by their own countrymen because of their not having taken extraordinary pains to recover the bodies of their slain for the purpose of interment. The notion seems to have been, that in the absence of appropriate burial, the shade of the dead one could not enter Hades, but was forced to wander disconsolately about the earth. But it was not, perhaps, so much for the ease of the wandering shade that the kinsfolk were moved to take due care of the dead body; for unless the shade were safely housed in Hades, it was in a position in its lonely wanderings to do harm, and would be inclined to do such harm, to those who had neglected to see that it was properly cared for.

REGILLA (page 53).

In the Blest Isles with him who rules austere

For an original and interesting treatment of an antique theme, see Edmund Gosse's beautiful and melodious poem, "The Island of the Blest," in his volume entitled "Firdausi in Exile and Other Poems." Homer, in the fourth book of The Odyssey, puts Rhadamanthus in the *Elysian Fields*. The passage is thus rendered by William Morris:

"But, Zeus-cherished Menelaus, to thee it shall not come
In the horse-kind land of Argos to meet thy death and doom.
But unto the fields Elysian and the wide world's utmost end,
Where dwells tawny Rhadamanthus, the Deathless thee shall send,
Wherein are the softest life-days that men may ever gain;
No snow and no ill weather, nor any drift of rain;
But Ocean ever wafteth the wind of the shrilly west,
On menfolk ever breathing, to give them might and rest;
Because thou hast wedded Helen, and God's son art said to be."

Pindar, on the other hand, in his second Olympian Ode, puts Rhadamanthus in the *Islands of the Blest*. The following is the passage as rendered in prose form by Ernest Myers:

"Then whosoever have been of good courage to the abiding steadfast thrice on either side of death and have refrained their souls from all iniquity, travel the road of Zeus unto the tower of Kronos: there round the islands of the blest the Ocean-breezes blow, and golden flowers are glowing, some from the land on trees of splendour, and some the water feedeth, with wreaths whereof they entwine their hands: so ordereth Rhadamanthus' just decree, whom at his own right hand hath ever the father Kronos, husband of Rhea, throned above all worlds."

Hesiod, in his *Works and Days*, treats of the Isles of

NOTES

the Blest in the following beautiful passage which is here given in the translation of the Rev. J. Banks:

"But when earth had covered this race also, again Jove, son of Cronus, wrought yet another, a fourth, on the many-nourishing ground, more just and more worthy, a Godlike race of hero-men, who are called by the former age demi-gods over the boundless earth. And these, baneful war, as well as the dire battle-din, destroyed, a part fighting before seven-gated Thebes, in the Cadmean land, for the flocks of Œdipus, and part also in ships beyond the vast depths of the sea, when it had led them to Troy for fair-haired Helen's sake. There indeed the end of death enshrouded them; but to them Jove, the son of Cronus, their sire, having given life and settlements apart from men, made them to dwell at the confines of earth, apart from the immortals. Among these Cronus rules. And they indeed dwell with careless spirit in the Isles of the Blest, beside deep-eddying Ocean; blest heroes, for whom thrice in a year doth the fertile soil bear blooming fruits as sweet as honey."

As to whether the ancient Greeks conceived the Elysian Fields and the Islands (or Island) of the Blest as being one and the same region under differing names, or as separate and distinct regions, or conceived the Elysian Fields as being in the Blest Isles, and so a part of them, is perhaps not easy to make out with any degree of certainty.

THE CHARIOTEER (page 55).

This Libyan bold deer to the Emperor's soul.

The word in the original here translated *Emperor* is *Autocrator*. Under the Eastern Empire, as Bury points out in his "History of the Later Roman Empire," Autocrater got to be used as an official title of the Emperor.

The second tercet of this sonnet is as follows in the original:

Et tu vas voir, si l'œil d'un mortel peut suffire
A cette apothéose où fuit un char de feu,
La Victoire voler pour rejoindre Porphyre.

A stranger, who is present at the games, and who is evidently seeking information as to the names, etc., of the contestants, runs across an adherent of the Blue faction of the circus, who is willing to gratify him, and who thereupon points out to him a great charioteer of that faction in the person of the son of Calchas, who is an illustrious Libyan and a favorite of the Emperor. While he is talking the race begins, but he still makes running comments, and at its close enthusiastically joins in the acclaim to the victor. Then in the language of extravagance, carried away by the exaltation of the moment, and being perhaps something of a poet, he exclaims to the stranger that if mortal eye can suffice for the blaze of so much glory he may see the goddess Victory in her car of fire again crowning Porphyry—the son of Calchas—as she doubtless had done more than once before. The scene might very well be laid at Constantinople during the reign of Justinian, who was not only a patron of the Blues, but was a frequent attendant on the games of the circus. Indeed, as we learn from Gibbon, the factions of the circus never before had raged as they did during his reign.

NOTES

FOR VIRGIL'S SHIP (page 59).

Thus Horace (excerpt from Ode III, Book I):

> Sic te diva potens Cypri,
> Sic fratres Helenæ, lucida sidera,
> Ventorumque regat pater,
> Obstrictis aliis præter Iapyga,
> Navis, quæ tibi creditum
> Debes Virgilium, finibus Atticis
> Reddas incolumem, precor,
> Et serves animæ dimidium meæ.

This is beautifully rendered by Lord Lytton as follows:

> So may the goddess who rules over Cyprus,
> So may the brothers of Helen, bright stars,
> So may the Father of Winds, while he fetters
> All, save Iapyx, the Breeze of the West,
>
> Speed thee, O Ship, as I pray thee to render
> Virgil, a debt duly lent to thy charge,
> Whole and intact on the Attican borders,
> Faithfully guarding the half of my soul.

Sargent renders the passage as follows:

> So may thy course the queen of Cyprus guide,
> So Helena's twin brethren light thy sails,
> And Æolus restrain all winds beside
> The North-west sweeping in propitious gales;
> That thou, O Ship, I earnestly implore,
> Mayst guard the precious freightage in thy care
> And through the billows to the Attic shore,
> Virgil, my soul's own half, in safety bear!

NOTES

It is interesting to compare with these the inferior version of Gladstone:

> So may the queen of Cyprian heights,
> So Helen's brethren, starry lights,
> So speed thy course the Lord of wind,
> And all, save Zephyr, fastly bind:
>
> O Ship, thou hast a debt to pay
> Our Virgil: hold him well I pray,
> Unharmed to Attic bounds consign,
> And save that life, the half of mine!

TO SEXTIUS (page 62).

Clear skies; the sands the boat has glided o'er;

Horace's Ode (Ode IV of Book I), which furnishes the basis for this sonnet, reads thus: "Trahuntque siccas machinæ carinas"—literally, And the machines [or engines] draw the dry keels [or boats]. That is, the vessels, which, during the winter, have been hauled upon the shore for safety, are, now that spring has come, drawn into the water.

GOD OF THE GARDENS—V (page 69).

In the fore-court the wax ancestors grace
I should grow old, and on their virile day
The children round my neck their bulla place.

The God, after lamenting his sad state and the fact that he is not treated with the same consideration as the Household Gods, ventures to suggest, that if he had his

NOTES

deserts he would be placed in the vestibule near the wax ancestors, where, as he grew old, the youths would devote their bullæ to him on their assumption at puberty of the toga virilis.

The vestibulum of the Roman house was, as is shown in Becker's Gallus, essentially a fore-court, and no part of the house proper. It was ornamented in various ways. It is related by Suetonius that in the vestibule of Nero's great house there was a colossal image of himself.

The Romans preserved the features of their ancestors in masks of wax, which they hung on the walls as we do family portraits. The wax was sometimes colored and the eyes represented by glass. We read that under the mask, in the old patrician families, were inscriptions indicating the name, the dignities and the great deeds of the deceased; and these portrait masks were connected in such a way as to indicate the genealogy of the family. This is illustrated as follows in the opening lines of Juvenal's eighth Satire. The translation is that of Gifford:

"Your ancient house!" no more.—I cannot see
The wondrous merits of a pedigree:
No, Ponticus;—nor of a proud display
Of smoky ancestors, in wax or clay;
Æmilius, mounted on his car sublime,
Curius, half wasted by the teeth of time,
Corvinus, dwindled to a shapeless bust,
And high-born Galba, crumbling into dust.

    What boots it, on the lineal tree to trace
Through many a branch, the founders of our race,
Time-honored chiefs; if, in their sight, we give
A loose to vice, and like low villains live?

NOTES

Say, what avails it, that, on either hand,
The stern Numantii, an illustrious band,
Frown from the walls, if their degenerate race
Waste the long night at dice, before their face?

* * * * * * * * * *

Fond man! though all the heroes of your line
Bedeck your halls, and round your galleries shine
In proud display; yet take this truth from me,
Virtue alone is true nobility.
Set Cossus, Drusus, Paulus, then, in view,
The bright example of their lives pursue;
Let these precede the statues of your race,
And these, when Consul, of your rods take place.

TEPIDARIUM (page 70).

And the pale daughters of Ausonia see

Ausonia was a name given by some of the poets to ancient Italy. See the seventh Æneid.

TRANQUILLUS (page 71).

And here with pointed stylus he has told,
Scratched in the unpitying wax, of him who tried
In Capri all that's foul when he was old.

It is scarcely credible that Tiberius could have led the life in Capri described with such disgusting detail in the pages of Suetonius.

NOTES

LUPERCUS (page 72):

Martial's Epigram in the original is as follows:

IN LUPERCUM

Occurris quoties, Luperce, nobis,
Vis mittam puerum, subinde dicis,
Cui tradas Epigrammaton libellum,
Lectum quem tibi protinus remittam?
Non est, quod puerum, Luperce, vexes
Longum est, si velit ad Pyrum venire.
Et scalis habito tribus, sed altis.
Quod quæris, propius petas licebit:
Argi nempe soles subire letum.
Contra Cæsaris est forum taberna,
Scriptis postibus hinc et inde totis,
Omnes ut cito perlegas Poëtas.
Illinc me pete; ne roges Atrectum:
Hoc nomen dominus gerit tabernæ
De primo dabit, alterove nido,
Rasum pumice, purpuraque, cultum,
Denariis tibi quinque Martialem.
Tanti non es, ais? sapis, Luperce.

The following translation may be ventured on.

TO LUPERCUS

When meeting me, how oft have you, Lupercus,
Asked, may I not my servant send unto thee,
To fetch that little book where brightly sparkle
Thy wondrous Epigrams the very latest,
Which, when I've read, I shall at once return thee?—

NOTES

But thus the boy you should not wish to harass;
For long, in truth, he'll find the road to Pyrum,*
And at my house three flights of steepy stairway.
Why go so far when near is all you wish for:
Of course you enter oft the Argiletum.*
Where, facing Cæsar's Forum, is a bookshop,
Whose posts are so becovered o'er with titles,
One may the poets quickly well examine.
There you should seek me; you may ask Atrectus;
His name's displayed full plainly as the owner.
From his first shelf or mayhap from some other,
With pumice smoothed and richly clothed in purple,
For five denarii he'll give you Martial.
Too much, you say? All wise are you, Lupercus.

AFTER CANNÆ (page 74).

The one-eyed Chieftain to their envious view.

Intermediate the battle of the Trebia and that of Cannæ Hannibal lost an eye as the result of an ophthalmia.

THE CYDNUS (page 79).

The dusky Lagian opes, in that charmed air,

Lagus (a Macedonian) was the founder of the dynasty to which Cleopatra belonged. Hence "la brune *Lagide*" of the original. Ptolemy, the son of Lagus, was the first of the so-called Macedonian Kings of Egypt.

ANTONY AND CLEOPATRA (page 81).

Only unbounded seas where galleys fly.

Alluding, of course, to the flight of Cleopatra's galleys at the battle of Actium.

---

*Pyrum was the region of Rome in which Martial lived, and Argiletum was a region famous for bookshops.

NOTES

EPIGRAPHIC SONNETS
(pages 85, 86, 87, 88 and 89).

The Roman cippus was used, among other things, for memorial inscriptions, as is illustrated in the headings to the sonnets on pages 85, 86, 87, 88 and 89. The "V. S. L. M." in three of these headings are the initial letters of the words, votum solvit libens merito—meaning that the vow [to erect the cippus] is gladly and deservedly fulfilled. These cippi were from the plainest to the most ornate in character.

A MEDAL (page 96).

Of all the tyrants whom a people hate,
Count, Duke or Marquis, Prince or Princeling d'en,—
Galeas, Hercules, Can or Ezzelin,—
None can the haughty Malatesta mate.

Galeazzo Maria Sforza, Duke of Milan (the Galeas of the text), was born in 1444 and died by assassination in 1476.

There were three sovereigns of the House of Este bearing the name of Hercules, one of whom was Duke of Modena in the eighteenth century. The two others were: Hercules I, Duke of Ferrara and Modena, who began his reign in 1471 and died in 1505; and Hercules II, Duke of Ferrara and Modena, who was born in 1508, and died in 1559, and whose mother was the celebrated Lucrezia Borgia.

There were three Cans who were sovereigns of Verona, their names being Can-Grande della Scala. The one

NOTES

mentioned in the text is doubtless the second one, of whom we read in Larousse that he was assassinated at Verona in 1359 by his brother Can-Signore, leaving behind him the memory of a rapacious and cruel tyrant. The most noted and best of them was the first one, who is familiarly known to us as Can-Grande, the friend of Dante. He sheltered the poet in his palace during a part of the time of his exile, and Dante gave him, on its completion, a copy of the Paradiso. In fact, it is thought there are several commendatory references to him in the Divine Comedy. It seems that an estrangement subsequently grew up between them. This Can-Grande was the Imperial Vicar, and was not only a great military leader, but a patron as well of letters and of the arts. He was born in 1291 and died in 1329, after a rule in Verona of nearly twenty years.

Ezzelino III is the Ezzelin mentioned in the text. He was known as the tyrant of Padua. He was born in 1194 and died in 1259. Plumptre, in one of his foot-notes to his translation of the twelfth Canto of Dante's Inferno, speaks of this Ezzelin as follows: "Of all the tyrants of that evil time, Ezzelin, known in popular legend as the Child of the Devil, was the most steeped in cruelties. Sismondi shrinks from telling the tale of his rapacity, his massacres, his fiendish tortures of his enemies. And his death was the fit close of such a life. Wounded and taken captive on his way to attack Milan, he was imprisoned at Soriano, refused all food and medical aid, sat for eleven days in gloomy silence, tore the bandages from his wound, and died." Dante puts him in the Seventh Circle of Hell with some other tyrants.

NOTES

On this Ezzelin, Eugene Lee-Hamilton has the following remarkable sonnet, to be found in his book of "Imaginary Sonnets":

EZZELIN TO LUCIFER
(1250)

The wolves were yelping round the castle tower;
  The witches croaked a baleful bridal hymn;
  The marsh lights danced all round the black moat's rim,
Where swam the moonlit snakes at spellful hour;

Like a hot whirlwind to my mother's bower,
  Then, Fiend, thou camest — scorching breast and limb
  With sulph'rous kisses, till the stars grew dim
And hungry Day did the thin moon devour.

O Lucifer, O Father, have I done
  Enough in thy dread service? Art thou pleased,
O pain-inflictor, with thy Paduan son?

Have I not turned my cities into hells?
  Foreburnt thy damned, innumerably teased
Men's feet with fire, and filled the world with yells?

The Malatestas, Lords of Rimini and of great part of the Romagna, began their career as sovereigns in the latter part of the thirteenth century and ended it in the early part of the sixteenth.

THE BEAUTIFUL VIOLE (page 100).

The original, from which the poet has taken for motto the first three lines, is as follows:

NOTES

D'UN VANNEUR DE BLÉ AUX VENTS

A vous trouppe légère
  Qui d'aile passagère
  Par le monde volez,
  Et d'un sifflant murmure
  L'ombrageuse verdure
  Doulcement esbranlez.

J'offre ces violettes
  Ces lis & ces fleurettes,
  Et ces roses icy,
  Ces vermeillettes roses
  Sont freschement écloses,
  Et ces œillets aussi.

De vostre doulce haleine
  Eventez ceste plaine
  Eventez ce séjour;
  Ce pendant que j'ahanne
  A mon blé que je vanne
  A la chaleur du jour.

This may be translated as follows:

FROM A WINNOWER OF GRAIN TO THE WINDS

Nimble troop, to you
  That on light pinion through
  The world forever pass,
  And with a murmuring sweet
  Where shade and verdure meet
  Toss gently leaf and grass,

NOTES

> I give these violets,
>   Lilies and flowerets,
> And roses here that blow;
> All these red-blushing roses
> Whose freshness now uncloses,
> And these rich pinks also.
>
> With your soft breath now deign
> To fan the spreading plain,
> And fan, too, this retreat,
> Whilst I with toil and strain
> Winnow my golden grain
> In the day's scorching heat.

Andrew Lang's beautiful version as taken from his "Ballads and Lyrics of Old France" (1872), is as follows:

HYMN TO THE WINDS

The winds are invoked by the Winnowers of Corn
Du Bellay, 1550.

> To you, troop so fleet,
> That with winged wandering feet,
>   Through the wide world pass,
> And with soft murmuring
> Toss the green shades of spring
>   In woods and grass,
> Lily and violet
> I give, and blossoms wet,
>   Roses and dew;

NOTES

This branch of blushing roses,
Whose fresh bud uncloses,
  Wind-flowers too.
Ah, winnow with sweet breath,
Winnow the holt and heath
  Round this retreat;
Where all the golden morn
We fan the gold o' the corn,
  In the sun's heat.

We are told that the poet accompanied his relative Cardinal Du Bellay to Rome in 1552, where he remained for nearly five years. Among his poems is a series of sonnets addressed to one Mademoiselle de Viole.

THE CONQUERORS (page 113).

Cipango's mines in rich perfection bear,

"Zipangu is a very large island on the east, and fifteen hundred miles distant from the shores of Mangi. The people of the island are of a white complexion and of gentle manners, and have a king of their own. They have gold in plenty, as few merchants resort thither, and no gold is allowed to be exported. Such as have traded to this island speak of the King's palace as being covered over with gold as our churches are with lead, and that the windows and floors are likewise of gold. It abounds in gold and is amazingly rich."—Travels of Marco Polo. Marco Polo does not pretend that he saw these things. Indeed, he says, "But I will now leave Zipangu, because I never was there, as it is not subject to the Khan." What he describes as having seen with his own

NOTES

eyes is now deemed to be veracious. Zipangu or Cipango is doubtless the modern Japan.

THE ANCESTOR (page 117).

Evidently descriptive of a portrait in enamel of the poet's ancestor by Claudius Popelin. The sonnet on page 107 celebrates Popelin's work in that field of art. The sonnets on pages 118 and 119 are in honor of this same ancestor — the founder of Cartagena.

Sierras, Terra Firma, Islands fair;

At this time the whole of South America was known by the name of Terra Firma.

TO A DEAD CITY (page 120).

Since Drake's fell heretics' rapacious raid
Thy lonely walls have mouldered in decay,
And, like some collar gloomed by pearls of gray,
Show gaping holes by Pointis' cannon made.

Drake captured Cartagena by assault in the latter part of the year 1585. Cates, of Drake's party, telling us that "in this furious entrée the Lieutenant-General slue with his owne hands the chief ensigne-bearer of the Spaniards, who fought very manfully to his life's end." The English kept possession of the place for six weeks, and then surrendered it on payment of a ransom of one hundred and ten thousand ducats, to which was added a thousand crowns for the surrender of the priory or abbey situated a short distance from the city. Cates deemed this ransom sufficient, "inasmuch as," among other reasons, "we have taken our full pleasure, both in the uttermost sacking and spoiling of all their household goods and merchandise, as also in that we have consumed and ruined a great part of their town with fire."—*Barrow's Life of Drake*, pp. 199-203.

Jean-Bernard Pointis, Baron de Desjeans, who was born in 1645 and died in 1707, was a distinguished naval officer of France. He had command of the expedition against Cartagena in 1697. He carried the city and was wounded in the attack upon it.

VISION OF KHEM—II (page 124).

Behind the Bari, which the priests convey,
Of Ammon-Ra, the sun's almighty head;

The Bari was a sacred boat in which the priests bore the image of a God or Gods. If on land, the boat was generally borne on the shoulders of the bearers. In the present instance the Bari, with the image of the God Ammon-Ra seated in it, is conveyed by the priests at the head of the imaginary procession.

"Ammon was the great God of Thebes, the southern Egyptian capital. According to Manetho, his name signified 'concealment' or 'that which is concealed'; and this meaning is confirmed both by the fact, which is now certain, that the root *amen*, in the hieroglyphics has the signification 'to veil,' 'to hide,' and also by statements in the religious poems of the Egyptians. We may therefore safely adopt the view of Plutarch, that the original notion of Ammon was that of a concealed or secret god, one who hid himself and whom it was difficult to find; or, in other words, that the mysterious and inscrutable nature of the Deity was the predominant idea in the minds of those who first worshipped God under this name. * * * Originally Ammon was quite distinct from Ra, 'the Sun,' no two ideas being more absolutely opposed than those of 'a concealed god' and of the great manifestation of Divine power and great illuminator of all things on earth, the solar luminary. But from the time of the eighteenth dynasty a union of the two Divinities took place, and Ammon was worshipped thenceforth almost exclusively as Ammon-Ra, and was depicted with the solar orb on his head."—*Rawlinson's Ancient Egypt*. This god became the head of the Egyptian pantheon, so that finally he was to the Egyptian what Zeus was to the Greek and Jupiter to the Roman.

Oscar Wilde, in his finely imaginative poem, "The Sphinx," sings thus of the God Ammon:

With Syrian oils his brows were bright: and widespread as a tent at noon
His marble limbs made pale the moon and lent the day a larger light.
His long hair was nine cubits' span and coloured like that yellow gem
Which hidden in their garment's hem the merchants bring from Kurdistan.
His face was as the must that lies upon a vat of new-made wine:
The seas could not insapphirine the perfect azure of his eyes.
His thick soft throat was white as milk and threaded with thin veins of blue:

NOTES

And curious pearls like frozen dew were broidered on his
 flowing silk.
On pearl and porphyry pedestalled he was too bright to
 look upon:
For on his ivory breast there shone the wondrous ocean
 emerald,
That mystic moonlit jewel which some diver of the
 Colchian caves
Had found beneath the blackening waves and carried to
 the Colchian witch.
Before his gilded galiot ran naked vine-wreathed
 corybants,
And lines of swaying elephants knelt down to draw his
 chariot,
And lines of swarthy Nubians bore up his litter as he
 rode
Down the great granite-paven road between the nodding
 peacock-fans.
The merchants brought him steatite from Sidon in their
 painted ships:
The meanest cup that touched his lips was fashioned from
 a chrysolite.
The merchants brought him cedar-chests of rich apparel
 bound with cords:
His train was borne by Memphian lords: young kings
 were glad to be his guests.
Ten hundred shaven priests did bow to Ammon's altar
 day and night,
Ten hundred lamps did wave their light through Ammon's
 carven house — and now

NOTES

Foul snake and speckled adder with their young ones
   crawl from stone to stone,
For ruined is the house and prone the great rose-marble
   monolith!
Wild ass or trotting jackal comes and couches in the
   mouldering gates:
Wild satyrs call unto their mates across the fallen fluted
   drums.
And on the summit of the pile the blue-faced ape of
   Horus sits
And gibbers while the figtree splits the pillars of the
   peristyle.

THE SAMURAI (page 128).

This was a man with two swords.

A fully equipped Samurai had two swords—a long one with which to do his fighting, and a short one for the hara-kiri.

THE DAIMIO (page 129).

Where burns its satin with a crimson sun.

The flag of Japan is white, with a large crimson disk in the centre.

THE CENTURY FLOWER (page 131).

Heredia, in this sonnet, has chosen to follow the erroneous notion, held by many, of the Century Plant not blooming until it has lived for a hundred years; and likewise, as is not unusual, he has confused the Agave

NOTES

with the Aloe. In fact, some of our dictionaries call the Agave the American Aloe.

On this subject Miss Alice Eastwood, of the California Academy of Sciences, has been kind enough to write me as follows:

"The Aloe of Belles Lettres, like the deadly Upas Tree, exists only in the imagination of the poets. It seems to be a combination of Agave or Century Plant, the Aloe, and probably a species of Cactus.

"The confusion arises undoubtedly from the similarity in manner of growth of the Agave and the Aloe. Both have thick, large, stiff-pointed leaves in a rosette at the surface of the ground from which the flowering stem arises. The Agave blooms generally in from ten to fifteen years. The flowering stalk at first resembles an immense green asparagus. It rapidly grows and soon reaches a height of from ten to twenty feet. It branches like a huge candelabrum, and the greenish flowers consist chiefly of the organs of reproduction. It belongs to the Amaryllis family. The Aloe sends up a comparatively slender stem, often curving gracefully, sometimes branching, and bearing numerous red, yellow or orange flowers in a spike or raceme, or sometimes densely clustered at the ends of branchlets. The flowers are tubular and about an inch long, usually pendent. It blooms often and belongs to the Lily family.

"Lowell, in 'A Fable for Critics,' alludes to the same superstition in the part beginning: 'Here comes Philothea,' etc."

Nor does the Century Plant bear a single flower, and

NOTES

that a scarlet one; on the contrary, it bears quite a number (I have counted as many as twenty), arranged in the fashion of a candelabrum and green in color, as pointed out by Miss Eastwood. The Century Plant, with its candelabrum of green blooms, is not an altogether unfamiliar object in the gardens of California.

The truth is, Heredia has treated, in this instance, for poetic purposes, one of the myths of the vegetable world, just as he has treated other myths in such wonderful manner in his other sonnets. And the poem is, indeed, beautiful, particularly in view of its suggested thought—the non-realization of our year-long hopes and dreams.

THE FUNERAL (page 136).

To Phocis' lustrous fanes as Pytho there,
Rock-bound and lightning-girdled, ruled alone.

Pytho was the ancient name of Delphi, the capital of Phocis. Hence the priestess who delivered the oracular responses at Delphi was called Pythia, and hence the games that were held near Delphi were called the Pythian games. The monuments at Delphi got to be of great magnificence. It is said that Nero took as many as seventy-five thousand statues from there to Rome.

BRITTANY (page 142).

Voluptuous Is and mighty Occismor.

Is and Occismor were two old cities of Brittany which were destroyed by extraordinary tidal waves near the middle of the fifth century.

NOTES

A FLOWERY SEA (page 143).

The inundation which seems to have furnished the subject of this sonnet may have been produced by a tidal wave of some such character as that which destroyed in old time the cities of Is and Occismor. In 1904, on the second of February, a tidal wave swept the coast of Penmarch, mentioned in the sonnet on page 149. One-third of the commune of Penmarch was submerged, and an immense amount of damage done.

ARMOR (page 148).

"Sell eus ar-mor."

This is in the Armoric dialect, and literally translated is, We have sight upon the sea; or, as we might say in English, Behold the sea! Armor is from *ar*, upon; and *mor*, sea—hence Armorica.

A RISING SEA (page 149).

Larousse, in his Universal Dictionary of the Nineteenth Century, says of the coast of Raz (mentioned in several of the sonnets): "La côte du Raz est extrêmement dangereuse, hérissée d'écueils longtemps funestes aux marins, jusqu'a l'établissement d'un phare construit il y a quelques années à côte d'un menhir. Le detroit (*raz en breton*) qui sépare le cap de l'Ile de Sein est d'une traversée extrêmement pénible, à cause d'un violent courant qui se porte entre le cap et l'Ile de Sein. De là l'adage breton dont voici la traduction littérale: *Jamais homme n'a passé le Raz sans avoir peur ou mal*.

NOTES

"C'est au moment d'une tempête qu'il faut visiter le bec du Raz," dit M. Pol de Courcy. "Quoique élevé de 72 mètres au-dessus de la mer, le promontoire semble à chaque instant prêt à s'engloutir sous les vagues; une écume salée vous couvre, et des rugissements horribles dans les cavernes des rochers étourdissent à donner le vertige."

(The coast of Raz is extremely dangerous, as it bristles with reefs which for a long time were fatal to mariners until the establishment of a lighthouse constructed some years ago near a menhir. The strait (raz in the Breton) which separates the cape from the isle of Sein is very difficult in the passage by reason of a violent current which runs between the cape and the isle of Sein. There is a Breton adage of which the following is a literal translation: *No man ever passed Raz without feeling fear or suffering harm.*

"It is at the time of tempest when one should visit the beak of Raz," says M. Pol de Courcy. "Although at an elevation of some 72 metres above the sea, it seems as though at each moment the promontory might be engulfed in the waves; a salted foam covers you, and the horrible roarings in the caverns of the rocks are so deafening as to make one dizzy.")

ON A BROKEN MARBLE (page 158).

The Sonnets of the Trophies, which begin with "Oblivion," very appropriately close with "On a Broken Marble" —the statue of the God Terminus in a state of wreck.

HEREDIA DEAD (page 161).

José-Maria de Heredia was born on the 22d day of November, 1842, on a coffee plantation (La Fortuna) in the Sierra Madre Mountains, near Santiago de Cuba, and died on the 3d day of October, 1905, at the Château de Bourdonne, in Seine-et-Oise, France.

His ancestry on the father's side is traceable to one of those daring Spanish Dons that made such famous and terrible history in the sixteenth century—his ancestor having been one of the founders of Cartagena. This is made brilliantly lustrous in the eight sonnets constituting the Conquerors' series of his Trophies.

His mother was a Frenchwoman, and at eight years of age he went to France for his education, which, having been partly achieved, he returned to Cuba for study at the University of Havana; but he subsequently returned to France for his permanent home, his residence having been taken up at Paris, where, in 1897, he was made librarian of the Arsenal Library.

As Edmund Gosse well says, he was no more Spanish than was Rossetti Italian.

His first verses were published in 1862, and from time to time there were publications of his in the *Revue des deux Mondes*, and other periodicals; but it was not until 1893 that his Trophies burst upon the world of letters in all the aggregation of their perfection and splendor.

At the first vacancy after this publication he was elected to the Academy, he having defeated Zola for that honor; nor has any challenge ever been made of the entire fitness of his selection, though the work which